MIDDLETOWN

MIDDLETOWN

a play

Will Eno

THEATRE COMMUNICATIONS GROUP
NEW YORK
2010

Middletown is published by Theatre Communications Group, Inc.,
520 Eighth Avenue, 24th Floor, New York, NY 10018-4156

Published under license from Oberon Books Ltd., 521 Caledonian Road, London N7 9RH.

This publication is made possible in part with public funds from the New York State Council on the Arts, a State Agency.

TCG books are exclusively distributed to the book trade by Consortium Book Sales and Distribution.

LIBRARY OF CONGRESS CATALOGING-IN-PUBLICATION DATA

Eno, Will, 1965–
Middletown : a play / Will Eno.—1st ed.
p. cm.
ISBN 978-1-55936-380-8
1. City and town life—Drama. I. Title.
PS3555.N652M53   2010
812'.54—dc22   2010035646

Book design and composition by Lisa Govan
Cover design by Mark Melnick
Front cover photographs: (top) The Granger Collection, NYC /
(bottom) Byron Barrett; back cover photograph: courtesy of the author

First Edition, November 2010
Third Printing, September 2014

To Gordon,
Mark,
and Cecile.

MIDDLETOWN

In death, Alexander of Macedon's end differed not a whit from his stable-boy's. Either both were received into the same generative principle of the universe, or both alike were dispersed into atoms.

—MARCUS AURELIUS, "MEDITATIONS"

There are two theories on hitting the knuckleball. Unfortunately, neither one of them works.

—CHARLEY LAU, BATTING COACH

We are born what we are, and if that was not lucky, we can make it worse with our thoughts. What the giant or dwarf thinks of, when he sees his reflection in the shopwindows while pretending to study the new spring styles, is a force in his life. A human being is not simply cells. There is a mind attached. This may often wish it had been born a tree.

—Gustav Eckstein

Mrs. Smith goes outside and screams, "It's the same outside as inside!"

—Gordon Lish, "Extravaganza"

Walter came by, this evening. We watched the new filly trying to stand in the twilight, with her legs so long and weak and funny. I told Walter my honest feelings about Europe and he did a magic trick. I hope my arm gets better. Lucy said, "Don't you find Walter very thin?" I said I liked him and it was nothing food could not cure. Tomorrow we hope for sunny weather. A French Horn expert is coming for a Presentation, and to have it outdoors in Great Field would be among other things an experience.

—Viola Kennebeck, "Diary," 1909

Prologue

PUBLIC SPEAKER: Ladies and Gentlemen, Esteemed Colleagues,
Members of the Board, Middletonians, Local Dignitaries,
everyone really, stockbrokers, dockworkers, celebrities,
nobodies, Ladies, Gentlemen, all comers, newcomers, the
newly departed, the poorly depicted, people who are still
teething, who are looking for a helping verb, the quote beautiful, the unquote unbeautiful, whose bones are just so, whose
veins are just so, the drunk, the high, the blue, the down, *los
pueblos*, *los animales*, foreigners, strangers, bookworms,
those whose eyes are tired from trying to read something into
everything, those at a crossroads, in a crisis, a quandary, a vel-
vety chair, the dirty, the hungry, yes, we the cranky, the thirsty,
the furious, the happy, who are filled with life, bloated with it,
gorged on words, and of course the bereaved, the bereft, and
let's not forget the local merchants, the smiling faces, the
placeholders, us, all we people slowly graying, slowly leaving,
who make all this all possible, this activity, this festivity, this

5

hope, this dream dreamt with open eyes, friends of the deceased, the diseased, friends of the disowned, and of course also healthy friendly people with great skin and congenital heart defects, sports fans, sufferers of autism, down-and-outers, nonbelievers, animal lovers everywhere, real people people, with doubts, without certainty, with nothing else worth mentioning, the majority of us, silent, stifled, delinquent, in the background, barely hanging on, running out of time, hope, air, heart, nerves, chances, money, blood, friends, courage, faith, hair, time, teeth, time, time, health, hope, all of it, all of it, those *sans* everything, those *avec* nothing, who can't stand it any longer, who never really could, gentle gentle people, infinitely injured people, lost souls, ghouls, ghosts, descendants, shades, shadows, future ancestors, Ladies, Gentlemen, I know I'm forgetting somebody, friends, likenesses, darknesses, citizens, people, hopeful people, hopeful people, everybody, every last lone dying and inconsolably lonely person, fellow human beings, breathing people, breathers, breathers . . . welcome. The fire exit's over there. I think you can also get out this way.

ACT ONE

———

Scene 1

Average evening. Middletown. Cop enters and strolls across the dimly lit stage. He comes to the window of a house, upstage. Through it, illuminated, Mrs. Swanson is seen unpacking boxes, hanging a painting on the wall, etc. Cop stands outside, looking in. He strolls a bit more, comes to another window of another house, upstage. Inside, John Dodge, illuminated, is seen sitting at a table, building a pyramid of playing cards. Cop stands outside, looking in. He strolls a little more, twirling his police baton. He approaches Mechanic, who is sitting on a bench, downstage, drinking out of a bottle in a paper bag. Mechanic eats something and throws the wrapper on the ground as Cop nears. Mechanic hurriedly hides the paper bag upon seeing Cop.

MECHANIC: Evening.
COP: Maybe. *(Referring to the bottle)* I saw that. You think I'm a cop. I look like a cop, I walk like a cop, so, you figure, case closed: I'm a cop.

7

MECHANIC: You're not a cop?

COP: No, I am a cop. You were right.

MECHANIC: Well, that's what I—

COP *(Interrupting)*: That's what you thought. <u>Everything is as</u> <u>everything seems, I guess. Good for everything.</u> What about you?

MECHANIC: What do you mean?

COP: What about you?

MECHANIC: I don't know. I mean, who knows, you know?

COP: No. What are you doing here?

MECHANIC: I was just walking around. Later tonight, I thought I might—

COP *(Interrupting)*: Forget about before and after. I mean now.

MECHANIC: Well, I don't know, because I was—

COP *(Interrupting)*: You don't know because you don't know. That's the trouble, the beauty, the trouble. So let's just leave it at that. *(Motioning to the wrapper Mechanic threw on the ground)* I think you dropped something. *(Mechanic picks up the wrapper)* The problem with people like—

MECHANIC *(Interrupting)*: I was just sitting here, minding my—

COP *(Interrupting)*: Don't interrupt.

(Long pause, as Mechanic waits and does not interrupt.)

MECHANIC: Was there something else you were—

COP *(Interrupting)*: I thought I said, don't interrupt. You know what, I should just goddamn . . . *(Long pause. To audience)* Welcome. Hi, hello. Welcome to the little town of Middletown. Ordinary place, ordinary time. But aren't they all? No. They are not, all. *(To Mechanic)* Say something nice.

MECHANIC *(To both the audience and Cop, with some unease)*: I'm just sitting here. I don't know what else. Um . . . *(He tries to think of something else)*

8

COP *(Pause. To audience)*: Right. Anyway, Middletown. Population: stable; elevation: same. The main street is called Main Street. The side streets are named after trees. Things are fairly predictable. People come, people go. Crying, by the way, in both directions.

MECHANIC: Ain't that the truth.

COP *(Immediately)*: Why don't you get out of here.

MECHANIC *(Defensively)*: Why? I'm not doing anything.

COP: And that's a reason you should stay? Let's go, move.

MECHANIC: Where?

COP: A different bench, I don't know, another perspective. Just not here, okay? In fact, you know what—here, allow me. *(Cop moves behind Mechanic and begins to choke him with his baton, pulling it with both hands against Mechanic's throat, from behind. Mechanic struggles, unable to breathe, unable to get free)* Say, "I'm not doing anything." Say, "I was just walking around." Say, "This is my hometown." Say, "My life's a mystery to me." Say it! Be a good human. Be filled with humility. With wonder and awe. Awe! *(Mechanic tries to speak, but is unable to breathe. Cop continues to choke him)* It's not easy, is it. Well, that's life. Listen, I'm sorry for what I'm still doing to you. Truly. But, don't worry. It'll be over in three, two, one . . . *(Cop continues choking Mechanic for three or four more seconds, and then releases him. Mechanic falls to the floor)* The floor is yours. *(Mechanic lies there for a moment. Then he gets up slowly, as he tries to breathe, tries to recover. He exits, shaken, and muttering something. To Mechanic)* Wonderful, great. *(Brief pause. To audience)* Excuse me. I'm not exactly sure what I was hoping to . . . I apologize. I was just trying to imitate nature. Anyway, welcome. Honestly. Middletown. *(Exits)*

Scene 2

Morning. The library. Librarian is at her desk, on the front of which is a sign that reads INFORMATION. Mrs. Swanson enters.

MRS. SWANSON: Good morning. I was hoping to get a library card.

LIBRARIAN: Good for you, dear. I think a lot of people figure, "Why bother? I'm just going to die, anyway." Let me just find the form. *(She looks through some paperwork)*

MRS. SWANSON: I wanted to learn more about the area. Do you have any books on Middletown?

LIBRARIAN: I should certainly hope so—let me take a look. *(She searches on her computer, believes for a moment that she's found something)* And . . . *voilà*. No, sorry, we don't. There's a wonderful book called *Yesteryear in Today's City of Tomorrow*. But it's out. It's due next Tuesday. *(Mechanic enters)* Hello.

MECHANIC *(Passing through. His voice is somewhat hoarse)*: Hi.

LIBRARIAN *(Searching on her computer)*: Here's something from the Chamber of Commerce, just to give you a general sense. *(She reads from the screen)* "Middletown was built on the ruins of other older Middletowns, and, before them, a town called Middenton, which was named for being between two other places, both unknown and now incidentally gone." *(Stops reading)* That doesn't sound right. "Incidentally gone." Anyway, *(She returns to reading)* "A thousand years ago, the area was home to the Chakmawg Indian and it was called Inpetway, which no one knows what it means, but it might have meant 'You are far away' or 'Between the snowing.' The Chakmawg had a highly developed culture and they thrived in their time, until they disappeared, forever. New residents arrived and looked around." *(Stops reading)* That's not much of a sentence. But I guess it still helps to give us a picture—people kind of lost and smiling. But, okay, let's see, *(She refinds her place in the text and continues reading)* ". . . arrived and looked around. Today, Middletown is a beehive, a human beehive, of activity and business. Many come to raise families and watch, swollen with civic pride, as their baby draws its first breath of local air. Also, drawn by the excellent clouds and the mostly silent nights, many come here to quietly retire. Middletown. We've got you coming and going."

MRS. SWANSON: That's from the Chamber of Commerce?

LIBRARIAN: I know. There's quite a lot they didn't mention. We have a great bike path. There's the library, here. And, of course, the people. Which is what most places are made out of, if you think about it.

MRS. SWANSON: I guess. I'll wait for that other book. *(Brief pause)* We just moved here.

MECHANIC *(Looking through a magazine, far from the Librarian's desk)*: I'm listening in on your conversation.

(Librarian and Mrs. Swanson briefly look over at Mechanic.)

LIBRARIAN *(To Mrs. Swanson)*: Sorry. You were saying?

MRS. SWANSON: My husband and I just moved here.

LIBRARIAN: Well, welcome. Is it just you two?

MRS. SWANSON: It's just us. He travels. But we're here now. I am. We're trying to start a family.

MECHANIC: "Come on, family—start! Start, you bastard!"

LIBRARIAN *(To Mechanic)*: Shhhh. *(To Mrs. Swanson)* Well, welcome to you both. That's wonderful. How long have you been trying?

MRS. SWANSON: Almost a year now.

LIBRARIAN: And I imagine it must be about the same for your husband. Well, good. Something you both can work on. Good for you. The world needs another person.

MECHANIC *(Again, from across the room)*: Whatever you do, don't have an only child. They're the worst. Or so I've been told. Every time you hear a little noise, some little singing or humming, you look over, and there it is again, the same only-child. *(Brief pause)* I'm just being me.

LIBRARIAN: Don't mind him, he's only . . . *(To Mechanic)* You're just responding to things around you, aren't you, dear.

MECHANIC: Basically. *(Very brief pause)* Hey, just did it again.

LIBRARIAN *(To Mrs. Swanson)*: Is there something else I can help you with? *(John Dodge enters)*

MRS. SWANSON: Do you have books on children? You must. On childbirth and children?

LIBRARIAN: We do. They're in the business section—I've never known why. I'll show you.

JOHN DODGE: Hi. Quick question. Books on gravity.

LIBRARIAN: Hi, John. *(To Mrs. Swanson)* Let me just get him squared away. One second. *(Searching on her computer. To John Dodge)* Books about gravity. Let's see. We have two: *The Silent Killer* and another one called *Laws of the World*.

JOHN DODGE: The second one.

LIBRARIAN: That just came back. Let me go see if it's sitting on a roll-y cart somewhere. *(Exits)*

MRS. SWANSON: Gravity. *(Brief pause)* Hello.

JOHN DODGE: Hi.

MRS. SWANSON: We just moved here.

JOHN DODGE: That's great. Who's we?

MECHANIC: They're trying to start a family.

MRS. SWANSON: Yes, we are, *(To Mechanic)* thank you. We is my husband and I. *(Mechanic drifts off. To John Dodge)* You live here, obviously.

JOHN DODGE: That I do. Is it obvious? Ten years, now. Ten, fifteen years. In fact, I think we're talking fifteen, twenty years, now. Time, you know? "Whooooosh." "Clank."

MRS. SWANSON: I guess. And what do you do?

JOHN DODGE: More like, what *don't* I do.

MRS. SWANSON: Okay, what *don't* you do?

JOHN DODGE *(Brief pause)*: You originally asked what *do* I do. So I'll answer that. I do paperwork, lawn work, plumbing, sometimes some house painting. I've worked graveyards, regular hours, happy hours. Sure, sometimes, I'll just stare out a window, let a year go by, two years. For instance, right now, I'm kind of between things. I'm between two crappy jobs, I'm sure—I just don't know what the second one is, yet. Give a call. I'm also trying to catch up on some reading. You might say I'm bent on self-improvement, although I'm sure there's a better phrase. *(Brief pause)* What about you? Wait, let me guess. *(A pause, perhaps five seconds, in which John Dodge stares at Mrs. Swanson and she waits for him to guess)* Yeah, I give up—no idea.

MRS. SWANSON *(Following the above line very quickly)*: I used to manage a restaurant. Before that I worked in a bank. Just jobs, you know. When we get settled, I might do something else.

JOHN DODGE: You sound like me.

MRS. SWANSON: No, I don't. I do?

JOHN DODGE: Sort of. Not really. I hate how I sound. You don't sound like me.

LIBRARIAN *(Enters, with book)*: Here we are. Speaking of gravity, you might be surprised to know we have a real astronaut from here.

MRS. SWANSON: I am. Wow.

JOHN DODGE: I bought a tandem bicycle from him. He was really friendly when I brought it back.

LIBRARIAN: Oh, he's a complete gentleman. He has one of those haircuts. He said he wouldn't be able to see us, way up there, but that he'd think about us. Can you imagine? All that splendor, all that wonder and beauty, and all you can say is just "Houston this" and "Houston that." To be so far away, with such a little vocabulary. *(She stamps the book for John Dodge)* And then there's John, here, with his handyman work and now his reading. Such *lively* people, our townspeople. Always trying different things. Always occupied, somehow. *(To Mrs. Swanson)* And now you, too. *(Hands John Dodge the book)* There you go. Bye, John.

JOHN DODGE: Thanks. Bye. *(To Mrs. Swanson)* Nice talking to you. Here's my card.

MRS. SWANSON *(Looks at it)*: This says "Lucy Graves Associates: If you need help, we can help."

JOHN DODGE: Yeah, that's wrong, that's someone else's card.

MRS. SWANSON: Okay. *(Pause)* Well, so, then, how would I get in touch with—

JOHN DODGE *(Interrupting)*: Here, why don't I just write my name and number on that one. *(He does so)* There we go. Problem created, problem solved. Bye. *(Exits)*

MRS. SWANSON: Bye.

LIBRARIAN *(To Mrs. Swanson)*: Now, you wanted books on children. What, specifically? "The history of . . ." or . . . I'm joking.

MRS. SWANSON: I thought you were. Health. Prenatal health. And also maybe wallpapering. We want to get a room ready.

LIBRARIAN: It's so exciting. A room. Wallpaper. I love the patterns. Little flowers or fire engines—it's almost too much. Let me show you. *(They exit)*

MECHANIC *(Moves downstage and stands very still, looking through the audience)*: I was nervous, earlier. I don't know why. Well, I do know—for part of it, I was being choked. And I'm nervous now, now that I think of it. But, I'm nothing special, postnatally speaking. I fix cars, I try to. I get hassled by the cops, try to maintain a certain—I don't know—sobriety. Sometimes, I volunteer at the hospital, dress up for the kids. It was part of a plea deal. But what isn't. Nothing really crazy to report. Except, I found this rock once, everyone. What I thought was a meteorite. I brought the thing into the school, here. The kids ran it through all these tests, tapped on it, shined lights at it. I found it in a field. It looked special. Then the astronaut here told me it was just a rock. Said it was probably from, at some earlier time, another slightly larger rock. His name is Greg Something. I had ideas about getting famous, getting on local TV with my meteorite. When it turned out to just be a rock, I thought I could still make some headlines with it if I threw it off a bridge, hit some family in their car and killed everybody. But then I figured, you know what, forget it, that's not me. So now some family's driving around, not knowing how lucky they are, not knowing how sweet it all is. Just because. *(Very brief pause)* Wait, hang on a second. Do you . . . *(Pause. He stays very still and listens intently)* I thought I heard something. *(Listens again for a moment)* I'm still not convinced I didn't. Weird. Anyway, that was just a little local story. Although, you know, it almost had outer space in it. *(Brief pause)* I wish that lady luck, with the family. People don't stop to think of how lucky they are. I do. And, I've realized, I'm not that lucky. But I get by. If I had more self-esteem, more stick-to-itiveness, I might have been a murderer. I was a child once. Like everybody. Some worried mother's son or distant father's daughter, sneaking around with a dirty face and an idea. My hand was this big. *(With thumb and forefinger he indicates the size of an infant's hand. About an inch and a half)* I was somebody's golden child, somebody's little hope. Now, I'm more just, you know, a local resident. Another earthling. *(Exits as Librarian returns to her desk)* Bye.

LIBRARIAN: Bye. *(To audience)* Hello. *(Phone rings. She holds up a finger, as if to say to the audience, "One moment." She picks up the phone)* Hello? *(Brief pause)* A book report on the Bible, okay. *(Brief pause)* We don't, no—no macaroni, no spray paint. We do have scissors and scrap paper. So you could probably— *(Very brief pause)* No, no glitter, either—you have to bring that, and you'll have to clean up. *(Cups her hand over the mouthpiece, to speak to the audience)* She's interested in writing a— *(Has to return to the caller)* Five o'clock. Okay. Bye bye. *(She hangs up. To audience)* That was a young child who—well, you probably heard. *(She returns to working at her desk. Lights down)*

Scene 3

Same stage set as in Scene 1. John Dodge's house and the Swanson house. Cop enters and strolls across the dimly lit stage, in the opposite direction of his earlier stroll. He speaks into his two-way radio.

COP: All units in the vicinity: see the man. See the man. See the woman. See the streets and houses, the shadows, the words that don't rhyme. All quiet here, over. No News is Good News, over. But there's no such thing as No News, over. Try to see my point. Just look at yourself, over. See the Universe. See a tiny person in the middle of it all, thrashing. See the bright side. Try to look at the bright side. *(Brief pause. To audience)* Sometimes I'll talk like this, over the wire. Just to see if anyone's listening.

COP'S RADIO *(Female voice)*: Someone's listening.

COP: Well, there you go. Now I know. *(Into two-way radio)* Hi, Susan. Sorry. All clear.

(He turns down two-way radio, puts it away, strolls. He comes to the window of John Dodge's house. He stands outside, looking in. John Dodge, illuminated, is inside, tossing a ball up and down, making notes. Cop strolls to the window of the Swanson house. Mrs. Swanson, illuminated, is inside reading. She stands, referring to her book and moving her hand over her belly. Cop turns to audience, moves downstage, as Mrs. Swanson and John Dodge move away from their windows. Gently:)

I do like this time of day: night. All the people. All their bones and arteries and personal problems. Beautiful animal: the Person. Dark. *(Pause)* I was too rough with that guy, earlier. I think I embarrassed him. Regrettable. I'm not myself. Sad stuff at home and I haven't been sleeping, but, I guess we all have a story. Once upon a time, Once upon a time, and so on, The End. *(Brief pause)* I try to uphold the law, keep some order around here, but, I have my moods. I just remember screaming "Awe" at the poor guy. Hard word to scream. It just sounds like a sound. And you can't bully people into feeling something, anyway. Oh, well. *(Pause. Mrs. Swanson and John Dodge, at staggered times, return to their windows)* We once almost had a Glass Museum, here. It would have been called the Middletown Glass Museum. Fact. *(Brief pause. He looks back toward the windows)* Behold. You know, just, look. This is what life is like, here, right now. *(Brief pause)* Looking in people's windows at night makes you feel lonely. Lonely, but, lonely along with the people in the windows. Along with the whole world, the whole lonely billions. It feels sort of holy, in some screwy way. Fact. *(Brief pause)* Fact.

17

Scene 4

Bright daylight. Town square. Tour Guide is holding a clipboard and some maps. She is standing before a simple block of granite, which measures four feet by four feet by four feet, and features a small plaque bearing an inscription in unreadably small letters. She checks her watch. A tourist couple arrives. Male Tourist has a camera hanging around his neck.

TOUR GUIDE: Morning. Are you here for the walking tour?

FEMALE TOURIST: We are. Hi.

TOUR GUIDE: Great. Hi. Have you done walking tours before?

MALE TOURIST: What time is it?

TOUR GUIDE: It's almost time. In fact, why don't we get going. Now, can either of you tell me what this is, that we're standing before? *(Pause)* No?

MALE TOURIST: It's a monument.

TOUR GUIDE: It's a monument, yes. To honor the founding of the town, here. The town of Middletown. So that we may never forget.

FEMALE TOURIST: Forget what?

TOUR GUIDE: Well, the history. The moment.

MALE TOURIST: We went to Rome, last summer.

FEMALE TOURIST: In search of eternal truth, and, to be totally honest, for the food.

TOUR GUIDE: I'd love to go to Italy. Rome is so old. I bet you saw some serious monuments there.

MALE TOURIST: The whole place is history. Old moments from here to Sunday.

FEMALE TOURIST: We walked everywhere. We saw all the famous things. A lot of the ancient inscriptions are chipped off or just kind of worn away. And they're in Latin, so even if they were readable, you can't really read them.

MALE TOURIST: It's a dead language.

TOUR GUIDE *(Referring to the monument)*: This is in English, so people can enjoy it for years to come.

FEMALE TOURIST: What about when English dies?

TOUR GUIDE: Oh, I think English'll be around for a pretty long time.

FEMALE TOURIST: I doubt the Romans thought Latin was going anywhere, either.

MALE TOURIST: We went to Holland, two summers ago. Holland was a world power, a glorious empire, ruthless. *(Brief pause)* We loved those "stroopwafels." They're, like, the local yummy snack. Ruthless empire; yummy snack. People change. Empires, too, is my point. So, ergo, I'm wary of monuments.

FEMALE TOURIST: He likes statues of horses, but, just the horse, no rider. Ergo . . . *(Small shrug)* you know?

MALE TOURIST: It's a magnificent animal: the horse. Just, incredibly noble. Listen, I used to gamble—the ponies, trotters. I kept scribbly notebooks and had big dark circles under my eyes. Lost my job, my previous wife—not a long story. But, anyway, yeah *(Gesturing toward monument)*, this makes me feel sort of sad and beautiful, sure, but not that sad and beautiful. *(Brief pause)* Look at us. No, really look at me and her. We've gone around the known world, lugging guidebooks and cameras. We've walked on crumbling Roman walls, ridden busses with chickens, taken ferries drunk at night over rough northern seas. *(Nodding toward Female Tourist)* She collects miniature spoons. Once, we rented a three-wheeled car.

FEMALE TOURIST: We're kind of on a quest. Just because we don't look like pilgrims doesn't mean we're not pilgrims.

MALE TOURIST: Spare us the speeches and brochures, if you could. We're in need, you know? Just, in a kind of quiet kind of normal need. I can see why you'd think we're just yahoos on vacation. But, we're serious people.

TOUR GUIDE: No, of course you are. *(Pause)* I'm not sure what you—I mean, I don't know . . . I give this tour every day. I'm normally thinking about lunch or looking for another job—I'm not really focused on the next ten thousand years. What can I say? It's just pretty regular, it's pretty everyday, around here. We don't have any other statu—

MALE TOURIST *(Interrupting)*: I'm not trying to be difficult.

FEMALE TOURIST *(Looking at monument)*: I sort of like it. It reminds me of my dad. *(They all look at it for a moment. To Male Tourist)* But I can see what you're saying. *(To Tour Guide)* I guess we kind of like a strange angle on things. If we go to the opera or something, sometimes we specially request Obstructed View seats. It somehow adds to the whole experience.

MALE TOURIST: And they're cheaper.

FEMALE TOURIST: We love a bargain. You know that saying, "Politeness doesn't cost you anything"? Sometimes, that's what we'll do for the weekend. Just go around being polite.

MALE TOURIST: We've saved a fortune.

FEMALE TOURIST: But, so, yeah, I guess we just like some perspective with our history. Some little, like, gossipy footnote about a local dish or a bastard child.

TOUR GUIDE: Sure, of course. *(Pause)* I grew up here. *(Referring to monument)* This thing was just always—I don't know— There. Or, Here. I trusted it was important. I'd see it in the rain and snow, serving its purpose. So that we remember, I guess. In general. So that we have memories.

FEMALE TOURIST: That's a thought.

TOUR GUIDE: I haven't traveled, ever. I'll walk around town, is about it. I'll notice a building or something, "Hey, was that always here?" Main Street, Elm Street. I look at people and try to figure out their story. You can sort of guess the first and last facts, but for the rest I'm just kind of, "What's going on inside of you?, because I have no idea." I don't know. I grew up here. I thought this was the world.

MALE TOURIST: Of course you did. But, hey, let me get a quick picture of you being wrong. *(He snaps a photo of Tour Guide)*

FEMALE TOURIST: We always sort of want something more, I guess because there's a long history of death in both our families. I guess we like things that are potentially monumental, but that aren't necessarily monumentalized, yet.

TOUR GUIDE: Well, then, I don't know— *(Looking around)* I guess then maybe that's everything else. Technically. *(Referring to the monument)* Other than this.

FEMALE TOURIST *(Interested in the possibility)*: Okay.

MALE TOURIST: Could be. Technically. Philosophically. Go on. *(He takes a photograph)*

TOUR GUIDE: For instance, the air. I wrote on it in school. Take a deep breath. *(They do)* A hundred years ago, someone was digging a hole here, for this very monument, and he rested on his shovel and sighed. You just inhaled a molecule of the air that shoveler exhaled, in that quiet sigh long ago. Scientific truth. And he, a hundred years ago, had just inhaled a molecule of air from Caesar's dying breath. Which dying breath probably contained a molecule from Caesar's first scream when he was born. Scientific fact. Molecules. Not the prettiest word. Everyone probably knows that Caesar thing. But still. *(Mrs. Swanson enters and stands near the group, wondering what's going on)* Think of how personal everything is, ultimately. And then, think of a beautiful sunset on Earth, before human beings had ever evolved. It just beautifully sets. No one there to say "Oooh" or "Ahhh" or something breathy like that. It just sets, and then it's night, nothing personal. *(To Mrs. Swanson)* Morning. *(To the group)* Beneath us, okay, the

21

dirt the sighing man was digging into? It's layers of fossils and broken pottery and things they think had religious value. Maybe some sad little instrument, way down, a hollow bone with three holes in it. Down we go. City, then dirt; town, then ash; village, then ice crystals and iron. Maybe a tooth or a piece of cloth. It's people strewn all the way through. And, people on top, too—walking around smiling and eating ice cream or doing whatever people do. *(Brief pause)* It's fun, thinking of everything like this. Usually, I'm telling people about the time sunglasses were almost invented here. *(Brief pause)* Some of the dust on my shoes is from outer space; most of the rest is dead human skin. Infinity, asteroids, and your great-great-grandmother. All that struggle and science and stale candy in every little speck. You look at it and you think, "Dirt." That's not even half the story. *(John Dodge enters, opposite side of the stage, carrying a plastic shopping bag. He stops and looks inside it, checks his pockets)* And there's a person, looking for something in a bag.

FEMALE TOURIST: It sort of completes the scene.

TOUR GUIDE: Sort of.

MALE TOURIST *(Taking a photograph of John Dodge)*: Look at him. Classic.

MRS. SWANSON *(Leaves the group, saying "hi" to them as she goes)*: Excuse me. Hi.

TOUR GUIDE *(To Mrs. Swanson, as she moves away)*: Hi. Bye. *(Brief pause)* There's a meadow we could walk to. Just nice grass and trees, nothing noticeably historical going on. The Chakmawg Indian believed trees were gods. They thought everything was. So that whatever you were doing, no matter what you were doing, you were praying. They had certain words you could only use when it was raining. They had a chant to heal people's hearts, another chant to keep the sky blue. What do you say? To the meadow?

FEMALE TOURIST: That sounds perfect. *(To Male Tourist)* Et tu, Brutus?

MALE TOURIST: Sounds good. Although, um, maybe a quick pit stop?

FEMALE TOURIST: Use your words.

MALE TOURIST: I need a bathroom.

FEMALE TOURIST: And maybe we can get a lemonade, somewhere?

TOUR GUIDE *(As they exit)*: Lemonade was invented in Pakistan.

FEMALE TOURIST: Really?

TOUR GUIDE: That's what they say. But I don't know how anyone could really know that.

Scene 5

Mrs. Swanson, who has been standing off to the side, perhaps trying to remember John Dodge's name, perhaps checking her hair, etc., approaches John Dodge.

MRS. SWANSON: John? We met at the library. You gave me your—

JOHN DODGE *(Interrupting)*: I remember. Sure. Hi. *(Still looking around)* I think I bought something and left it at the store. That wasn't a very smart investment.

MRS. SWANSON: I've done that—it's so stupid. Hey, are you hungry? *(She sits down on a bench)* I have some little sandwiches. I'm really hungry.

JOHN DODGE: That'd be great. *(Still thinking about whatever he lost)* Damn it! *(Brief pause)* I'm sorry—I would love a sandwich. *(He sits)* Thanks.

MRS. SWANSON: Was that a tour going on?

JOHN DODGE: I'm sure it was something. *(Brief pause)* God, I had the worst night. Almost nonstop meaningful silence. Worst morning, too. Don't get married, that's my advice.

MRS. SWANSON: I'm already married.

JOHN DODGE: Oh, that's right, I forgot. Well, I hope you brought a good book.

MRS. SWANSON: I didn't know you're . . . Are you married?

JOHN DODGE: I was. All I remember is lying in bed, listening to the breathing. That's not true. We had some pretty good times. Probably my best. Yeah.

MRS. SWANSON: I'm sorry.

JOHN DODGE: It's sad. You sit around reading the side of a cereal box. Half the dishes are gone, half the cups, you eat everything out of a dented can, no more pretty shoes by the door, and, that's your little half-life. *(Brief pause)* Whatever you do, don't get divorced. I know, I'm all over the place on that one. *(Brief pause)* Sorry. Are you getting settled here?

MRS. SWANSON: I am. We are. More and more. This is all a big change.

JOHN DODGE: What?

MRS. SWANSON: Here. And the whole idea of children.

JOHN DODGE: It is. I have two nieces.

MRS. SWANSON: Oh, how great—girls.

JOHN DODGE: They are great. You know what—it's just one niece, I think. The other one is her friend. I'm a terrible uncle. But, I don't know, I still feel like a nephew. Time, you know. "Buzzzzzzz." "Plink."

MRS. SWANSON: You said that the day we met.

JOHN DODGE: Something like it, I'm sure. It's a theory of mine.

MRS. SWANSON: It's not really a theory. You're just making different sounds with your mouth.

JOHN DODGE: So are you.

MRS. SWANSON: True. "True." *(Brief pause)* How's gravity?

JOHN DODGE: It's all right, I guess. *(Brief pause)* What?

MRS. SWANSON: You were reading a book about gravity.

JOHN DODGE: Oh, right. That's over. I just kind of lost the . . . you know. I mean, do I really need to know about that? Anyway, now, I'm taking this course on watercolor painting.

MRS. SWANSON: You're quite a Renaissance man.

JOHN DODGE: It's not really a course. It's just the directions that came with the paints.

MRS. SWANSON: Well, still, it sounds great.

JOHN DODGE: It's not. It's just some other thing.

MRS. SWANSON: I would think you'd make a really good uncle.

JOHN DODGE: I would, too, but, yeah, no. I get, I don't know— I panic. So I'm no good as an uncle. Who wants a panicky uncle? I don't know. I get anxious, you know? I forget everybody's name and birthday and get all nervous and worried I won't recognize people.

MRS. SWANSON: I feel that way sometimes.

JOHN DODGE: Me, too.

MRS. SWANSON *(Brief pause)*: So, Bob is finishing up some things with work and our old house. He just started up in a new position. He should be here soon. I still don't really know the place. It can get lonely, can't it.

JOHN DODGE: Yeah. You get the mail, it's a clothes catalog. Maybe you leaf through it, maybe think, "Hey, I could buy those pants." Then you think, "But then it'd just be me, again, in a different pair of pants." Then you go out and walk around, and that's your day, time for bed.

MRS. SWANSON: That's kind of gloomy. I like looking at catalogs. Things aren't so bad. I visit Bob here and there, if he's at a convention or something nearby. He's in sales.

JOHN DODGE: I always wanted to be in something.

MRS. SWANSON: Yeah? Well, I'm sure you'll, you know . . .

JOHN DODGE: Yeah? That's nice. Thanks.

MRS. SWANSON *(Brief pause)*: I've been having trouble sleeping.

JOHN DODGE: Oh God—nighttime. Daytime, too. I'm like, "Enough—I get it." *(Brief pause)* I read articles about identity theft and I actually get a little jealous, you know? "Just take it," you know. "Good riddance." Sometimes, I think I might just go quietly retire, you know, alone in the bathroom, with an X-acto knife. But then I start up some dumb project or get a book about some idiot thing.

MRS. SWANSON *(With real sympathy)*: John.

JOHN DODGE: You have a nice voice, um . . . I'm sorry . . .

MRS. SWANSON: Mary.

JOHN DODGE: Mary, of course. I like it.

MRS. SWANSON: We all have our dark nights. We're probably never as alone as we think.

JOHN DODGE: Yeah, no. We hope. *(Brief pause)* I heard what you said. It probably seemed like I didn't, but I did. I'm really sorry you can't sleep.

MRS. SWANSON: Me, too. No . . . thank you. *(Moved, by even this very small kindness)* I know you're just making sounds with your mouth again, but, thanks.

JOHN DODGE: I haven't asked you a lot about yourself.

MRS. SWANSON: Is that . . . are you asking now?

JOHN DODGE: No, or, I don't know—I just suddenly tried to picture you not sleeping. Sometimes you get used to the words for things, and then you suddenly remember the things. And so I suddenly saw you, the real Mary, not a word, staring out a window, or crying or reading, whatever you do.

MRS. SWANSON: I do read, sometimes. Or, yeah, sometimes, cry. That's nice of you to—it's nice you would picture me. In tears, or reading. *(Brief pause)* Night is hard, you know? It gets so quiet. I never know what I'm supposed to be listening to. *(Brief pause)* But it does give me time to catch up on my needless worry.

JOHN DODGE *(Small laugh)*: I do that—what you just did.

MRS. SWANSON: What?

JOHN DODGE: Use humor to try to distance myself from the pain.

MRS. SWANSON: I was using humor to try to be funny.

JOHN DODGE: Yeah, no, that's something different. *(Brief pause)* If you ever need any help, I'm pretty good with the needless worry.

MRS. SWANSON: The other night, I couldn't stop thinking, "What if my taste buds stop working?"

JOHN DODGE: Massive heart failure in a public place.

MRS. SWANSON: You can do better than that. Plus, that's really more of a guy thing.

JOHN DODGE: Cancer, in the privacy of your own home.

MRS. SWANSON: Now you're talking. The old standby. And, yes, good—something for the ladies.

JOHN DODGE *(Without having laughed)*: It's good to laugh. *(Brief pause)* I like that thing you said—"dark nights."

MRS. SWANSON: I guess all nights are dark, but you know what I mean. *(Brief pause)* Oh, I almost forgot. I'm hoping you can come have a look at something.

JOHN DODGE: I'd love to. What?

MRS. SWANSON: A plumbing thing. I think it's just a clogged drain.

JOHN DODGE: I was thinking maybe it was a painting or a sunset or something.

MRS. SWANSON: No. *(Small smile)* Sorry.

JOHN DODGE: Yeah, I'll take a look. I could use the work. Not that I'd charge you. *(He gets up)* Speaking of not making any money, I should get going. Hey, what's today?

MRS. SWANSON: Tuesday. *(Or whatever the actual day is)*

JOHN DODGE: Oh, shit. I thought it was Monday. *(Or whatever the actual day before would be)*

MRS. SWANSON: Sorry, again.

JOHN DODGE: I would have found out eventually.

MRS. SWANSON: I'll give you a call. Bye, John.

JOHN DODGE: Bye, Mary. It was really nice talking.

MRS. SWANSON: It was. Thank you. We should—yes. Definitely. Bye, see you later.

(He exits. She begins to exit, then sits back down, as the lights fade.)

Scene 6

Lights suggest evening. Librarian, with her purse and some books, enters.

LIBRARIAN *(To audience)*: That book came back today. I was just reading. Here: *(She reads, periodically clarifying terms for the audience)* "Life had gone on. Several moons had passed." *(Clarifying)* Several months. *(She reads)* "The medicine man"—a medicine man is a doctor—"The medicine man shook his feathers. The villagers stood, shivering. A star shone over Inpetway." That's here. It was. *(She reads)* "The medicine man spoke in difficult ways of difficult things, in the worried vocabulary of medicine and night. The villagers listened quietly, and quietly misunderstood. The sick man listened, and quietly got worse." For "sick man," just think of anybody, an average person. A child has written in the margin here: "anxiety, sickness, death, spiritual." *(She quickly shows us)* She writes in these wonderful loopy letters in a bright red pen. At least, I think it's a girl. *(She reads)* "The medicine man continued—differently, now. His calm eyes sparkled slowly, as he turned to the blushing woman there." The "blushing woman" is probably a bride or a woman falling in love. *(She*

28

reads) "He spoke now in simple ways of simple things. He asked the moon to be beautiful. He asked the sun to come to warm the unborn child and the born mother. He asked the people to be human and the animals to stay animals. He asked the Universe to expand. He said, deeply, to all of them, 'Great things. Oh, Great things. Someone is born, someone will die, both are you. Unwind, unknow.'" The same little girl has written a question mark, here. *(Brief pause)* I read once the question mark comes from a musical notation used in Gregorian chants, to signal that the phrase should have an upward intonation, that it should rise upward, to Heaven. Imagine this little red one here—no sentence, no question, just a little red question mark, by itself—rising up to Heaven, to God. Imagine the look on His face. *(Leafing forward a few pages)* Later, she's written the word "atmosphere." And here's a barrette she used for a bookmark. Ah, literature. *(Brief pause. Looking up)* It's a beautiful night. Whether or not there's anything up there.

Scene 7

Greg is seated in a chair, tilted sideways, facing the audience. He is in a space capsule, floating. The following lines are amplified, with some static and perhaps some delay, as though a radio transmission. Ground Control may be seated onstage, perhaps facing away from the audience.

GROUND CONTROL: Cormorant Nine. *(Pause)* Cormorant Nine. This is Ground Control, Houston. Do you read? Do you copy?

GREG: This is C-9. Copy. Sounds like you're in my living room. Over.

GROUND CONTROL: The things we can do. Go ahead, C-9. How's life?

GREG: What a view, is one thing. I've heard about it. But, what a wonderful . . . I never knew how round round was, Houston. God. All this space, it's just pure majesty, it's endless, majestic. But it's cold, it's almost just raw data, raw mathematics. Then you see little planet Earth and—my God, she's just so welcoming and good. Seems like a symphony should be playing. It, wow, it's just this beautiful fragile thing, something a happy child would draw. It's so blue. Houston.

GROUND CONTROL *(Indistinct sentence, something like: "Fivv—. Gull sensor. Ooh min. Ive.")*

GREG: Repeat, please.

GROUND CONTROL: Fifty-one degrees. Angle sensor arm, two minutes forty-five.

GREG: Copy. Arm is in position. *(A short indistinct sentence)*

GROUND CONTROL: What's that? Didn't catch that.

GREG *(Pause)*: Sorry?

GROUND CONTROL: Go ahead, Greg.

GREG: Oh. I'm just trying to picture life, back home in the old hometown. Down there in Middletown. There's a guy there I remember, thought he found a meteorite, once. It was normal sedimentary rock, just made from dead animals and plants crushed together. He was disappointed. Shouldn't have been. I was never crazy about him, I think he bashed my mailbox in, but, he shouldn't have been sad. That rock, that guy who found it, the field he found it in, all these things are miraculous because all these things are earthly. The words he used to refer to it, the breath it took to make the words, all of it. Just sacredly and profoundly and mysteriously—well, yeah—earthly.

GROUND CONTROL: Are you getting mystical on us, Greg?

GREG: I'm just looking and talking, Houston. I didn't prepare anything.

GROUND CONTROL: Just giving you a hard time, partner.

GREG: Okay.

GROUND CONTROL: Looking good. Go ahead.

GREG: I'm done. But I just have to say, it doesn't look lonely from up here. Everything looks right-next-door. It's where you're sitting, right now. How 'bout that. You're breathing the Earth's atmosphere. You got mountains and clouds, oceans. People out doing things together. Soccer games and birthday parties, listening to beautiful music. Inexpressible, you know. How'd we get so lucky? *(Brief pause)* I probably sound like a real cliché. Me, with my chiseled features and the flight suit, waxing all poetic. Waxing all fragile and religious.

GROUND CONTROL: All right, Greg. *(Brief pause)* Synchronize, one seven six.

GREG: Synchronize, one seven six.

GROUND CONTROL: Copy. *(Pause. Some garbled static)* Say again, Cormorant Niner?

GREG: I didn't say anything. Go ahead, Houston.

GROUND CONTROL: Roger. No matter. Looking good. We do recommend P65 alignment, plus point two two.

GREG: Thank you—P65, plus point two two. *(Brief pause)* I'm looking out at the world. I'm thinking about people. I can't tell you what this is like. Over.

GROUND CONTROL: Copy.

GREG *(Mouths the words: "Maybe everybody knows exactly what this is like," without making any sound at all.)*

GROUND CONTROL: Wunderbar, Greg. Looking good. We have no abnormalities. Over.

(Static. Static fades.)

Scene 8

The Swanson kitchen. John Dodge is working on the kitchen sink drain. He is lying on the floor, periodically ducking in and out of the cabinet, and therefore periodically inaudible. At the top of the scene, he is on his back, his head and upper torso hidden in the cabinet. Mrs. Swanson is at the kitchen table.

MRS. SWANSON: Where's John? Where did he go? No, seriously, John, thanks for helping out. Bob and I are grateful.

JOHN DODGE *(Appearing from under the sink to grab a wrench)*: No, it's no trouble. When does he get here?

MRS. SWANSON: Any day, I hope. It's crazy. We used to just be regular people. We said "good night" and "good morning" every day. All of a sudden we're so modern. It's funny. *(Brief pause)* Have you always done this kind of work?

JOHN DODGE: God, yeah. In fact, I've been thinking about that philosophy thing about how you can't step in the same river twice. It turns out you can. Sometimes, I feel like I should just . . . I don't know. I try, you know, but some days it all just seems like the—— *(Disappears under the sink. Indistinct end to the sentence)*

MRS. SWANSON: I know. I know what you mean. Everything suddenly looks like it's spelled wrong, or something. Like, even your own name looks like a typo.

JOHN DODGE *(Appearing)*: Yeah, exactly. I'm always getting, I don't know, I told you this, I get these awful panic attacks. They're actually how I stay in shape. It's a mess. Enough about me, and how I sometimes get claustrophobia and can't swim. *(Indistinct short question, an indecipherable version of: "So how does it feel being pregnant?")*

MRS. SWANSON: What?

JOHN DODGE *(Repeating mainly as before.)*

MRS. SWANSON: Oh. It's so new. I don't think I could even describe it. I'm really excited. But it's almost like it's just words, at this point.

JOHN DODGE *(Indistinct medium-length sentence, an indecipherable version of: "It's probably just words at every point.")*

MRS. SWANSON: You're probably right—it's just words at every point. It scares me, though. Having a baby. The words seem so tiny and quiet, compared to the truth of it. Compared with if you really try to picture it. Not to mention, just, the whole thing. I mean, do I look like the kind of person?

JOHN DODGE *(Indistinct medium-length sentence, an indecipherable version of: "Well, I don't know if you're the kind of person, but I think you're quite intoxicating.")*

MRS. SWANSON: Well, thank you, John. I don't think I've ever been called "intoxicating" before. That's very flattering.

JOHN DODGE: I hope you don't think of me as just some kind of a . . . I don't know. Because I have so much going on inside me. A lot of different . . . *(Brief pause)* You know, people laughed when I said I wanted to get a law degree.

MRS. SWANSON: You have a law degree?

JOHN DODGE: Me? Oh God no. People really laughed, though. *(Brief pause)* I've wanted a lot, out of life. First, air and milk, and then it just kept going.

MRS. SWANSON: Well, you've gotten a lot, too, haven't you? In life?

JOHN DODGE: I had shingles, once. I'm kidding. Well, no, I'm not, actually—I did have that. Good argument for death, by the way—shingles. Nice reminder your skin's an enemy.

MRS. SWANSON: Your skin's probably your best friend.

JOHN DODGE: For a while, sure. *(Very brief pause)* I have a kind of serious mind/body problem. But, I know what you're saying. I try to be grateful for what I have.

MRS. SWANSON: Good. I wish I had more gratitude. When you think of all the miracles it takes just to sit in a chair. A billion things going right, just to sit here. And do nothing. And watch you work. Miracles.

JOHN DODGE: You get used to them, though. That's the sad thing. You look around: miracle, miracle, miracle. It's tiring. It's sad. Or scary. *(Indistinct short sentence)*

MRS. SWANSON: That's kind of extreme, isn't it? But, I guess, to be completely honest, it's always an option.

JOHN DODGE *(Indistinct short sentence, indecipherable version of: "Except for the fact that I'm afraid of dying.")*

MRS. SWANSON *(Laughing)*: You can say that again. Oh, Johnny Boy, you can say that again.

JOHN DODGE *(Appearing)*: That "I'm afraid of dying"?

MRS. SWANSON: I thought you said something different.

JOHN DODGE: No. *(He removes a handful of sludge from the drain, puts it onto a piece of newspaper)* There.

MRS. SWANSON: Yuck. Is that the problem?

JOHN DODGE: Yeah.

MRS. SWANSON: What is it?

JOHN DODGE: Just years of stuff. Sort of a metaphor for, yeah, no— just years of stuff, gunk. *(He stands up. He is dizzy)* Whoa. I stood up too quick. My whole life, I don't think I ever stood up at the right speed. All life long, John Dodge in the wrong. "All life long," wow, that's hard to say.

MRS. SWANSON: No it isn't.

JOHN DODGE *(Effortlessly)*: "All life long." No, you're right—it isn't. I think I better sit down for a few seconds. *(He sits down)* One one-thousand, two one-thousand, three one-thousand. Okay. *(He stands up, is dizzy again)* Wow. Did it again. *(Leans on the table)*

MRS. SWANSON *(She takes his hand, briefly)*: Maybe you're just a dizzy person. They say some people have trouble with the Earth's, you know, with the rotation.

JOHN DODGE: Yeah, maybe that's—yeah. *(Brief pause)*

MRS. SWANSON: John.

JOHN DODGE: Again, she says, in her nice voice, "John."

MRS. SWANSON *(Small slightly nervous laugh)*: Well, what am I supposed to say? *(Brief pause)* Are you all right? *(Very brief pause)* We haven't known each other very long, but, do I seem different?

JOHN DODGE: How?

MRS. SWANSON: I don't know. Somehow. Inside.

JOHN DODGE: Yeah, I don't know. Kind of. Yeah, you do.

MRS. SWANSON *(Small smile)*: Good.

JOHN DODGE: Change.

MRS. SWANSON: I know.

JOHN DODGE: You smiled when you said: "Good." That says a lot about you. You look really well. I bet you'll be a radiant mother. *(Pause)* I don't have anything, Mary. Sorry, big change of topic, but—I don't. Look at me. I have a bunch of hobbies I quit and some overdue books I never read. I don't have anything.

MRS. SWANSON: Yes, you do. Come on. Yes, you do.

JOHN DODGE: Mary, I don't.

MRS. SWANSON: Maybe you're not looking hard enough.

JOHN DODGE *(Short indistinct sentence, somewhat clearly vocalized)*: Mome gavnerma thurn.

MRS. SWANSON: What?

JOHN DODGE: Just joking, because of the— *(He points to the cabinet)* Remember when you couldn't hear me?

MRS. SWANSON: Oh, right. *(She covers her mouth and says an indistinct line, about five syllables long, perhaps something like: "Gabralldee yo fon gerg fonderall.")*

JOHN DODGE: Hmm. I never thought of it that way. *(They share a little laugh. Very brief pause)* Seriously.

(Lights down. Mrs. Swanson and John Dodge remain, for a moment.)

Scene 9

Cop enters darkened stage with powerful flashlight. Behind him, Intermission Audience enters and is seated, facing the actual audience. Cop shines his flashlight into the face of an actual audience member. He moves the light to another audience member, and then another.

COP: Don't worry. People always look so worried. *(Shines light around the audience)* We got a report of some problem, down here. Some trouble. A scream, maybe a loud sigh, a couple of sighs, something. I'm sure it's fine. Just normal people being human in the night. Inner life meeting outer life. Bang. Kapow. But, yeah. Nothing to worry about. *(He shines the light back over the stage)* Sleep tight, pretty Middletown. All is well. *(Flashlight goes out. He bangs it on his leg a couple of times. It comes back on)* There we go. *(Brief pause)* Okay. Pray the Lord your soul to keep. Something like that. Whatever makes you feel calm. *(Brief pause)* Just be all right. *(Exits)*

Scene 10

The intermission of this play. Lights that suggest house lighting come up. Recorded applause. The Intermission Audience, seated onstage, applauds.

Intermission Audience is made up of Freelancer, Man and Woman (on a date), Sweetheart (a girl with a mild mental disability) and her Aunt. Some have programs for Middletown. *Almost all of Sweetheart's lines are said very loudly, but not shouted. Freelancer is writing in a notebook.*

AUNT *(Brief pause)*: I should have brought a sweater. Are you cold, Sweetheart?

SWEETHEART: Feelings.

AUNT: Remember, we're inside. *(To others)* Excuse me. *(To Sweetheart)* Would you like some candy?

SWEETHEART: "What about when English dies."

AUNT: Nice and quiet, dear. *(Gives Sweetheart some candy)*

FREELANCER: That's from the play. *(He writes)*

MAN *(Standing and stretching)*: Excuse me. *(Exits)*

AUNT *(To Freelancer)*: You're very busy.

FREELANCER: I'm writing a book on being an audience member. Originally, I wanted to be an autobiographer.

AUNT: Oh?

FREELANCER: Yeah. But then I had to sit down and ask myself, "Seriously? Me?"

AUNT: What do you like to go see?

FREELANCER: Oh, God, anything and everything. I've seen horses being born, Egyptian tombs being exhumed. I've gone whale watching, I watched my poor mother die, saw a Hindu bathing festival, a total solar eclipse, you name it. Mainly plays. Sometimes, I have anxiety attacks when the curtain goes up.

WOMAN: I always want to cry at the end. When you see the actors smiling and bowing in the light. Dead kings waving to their wives and girlfriends.

SWEETHEART: "I'm just passing through."

FREELANCER: That was in there, too, right at the beginning. I have the worst memory. But I like to write down lines. *(Writing down the line. To Aunt)* Your daughter has an amazing memory.

AUNT: She certainly does. She's my niece.

FREELANCER: Well, she has a very good memory. *(To Sweetheart)* What's your first memory, ever? *(Long pause. No response from Sweetheart)* It's hard, isn't it. *(Brief pause)* I was always sitting somewhere. I was born in the audience.

AUNT *(Brief pause)*: I like when plays have a break in the middle. Once we met an oceanography student. *(To Sweetheart)* Remember, he painted the garage? It's nice.

FREELANCER: It's funny, though. Since you don't know the end, you're not sure what you're in the middle of. Hey. *(Pleased with the thought, he writes it down)*

MAN *(Enters)*: Much better. Are we talking about the play? Let me ask, so the town is like a—

AUNT *(Interrupting)*: The town is called Middletown. But it has other names.

MAN: Yeah, I got that. But the people are—

AUNT *(Interrupting)*: I think the main two are having a romance. They represent the future, I think.

MAN: Thanks. I really enjoyed that.

WOMAN: I had a neighbor like the John guy. If you talked to him, he would listen so hard, but you weren't sure what he was listening to. He finally left or something bad happened. It was really sad. He didn't have anybody. At least, the guy in the play has the lady who just moved in.

AUNT: Mary.

SWEETHEART: "Houston."

AUNT *(To Sweetheart)*: Houston is in Texas.

SWEETHEART: "Your daughter has an amazing memory."

FREELANCER *(Standing, stretching)*: My back is killing me. I think it's growing into the shape of a chair.

SWEETHEART: "I have the worst memory."

WOMAN *(Brief pause)*: You know what's funny? So, everything, in a way, is still going on. Time's going by, in the town, at the library, in outer space, here—all over. In a fictional way, of course, but, at the same time, like, nonfictionally, too.

MAN: Relativity.

WOMAN *(Brief pause)*: Is that your contribution?

MAN: Yeah. Just, everything's all, I don't know——Sir Albert Einstein.

WOMAN: I don't think he was ever knighted, but, okay. *(To Aunt and Freelancer)* But, do you know what I'm saying? Something's coming.

AUNT: But we don't know what.

WOMAN: Neither do they. They're right in the middle of some life in some town—you know, in a way.

AUNT: They deserve something good. We all do.

SWEETHEART: "Life."

AUNT: It's quite a topic, isn't it. I think she's pregnant, Mrs. Swenson. There's always a glow, a kind of shadow. You can tell.

FREELANCER: It's always a possibility.

MAN: So is suicide.

WOMAN: Where did that come from?

MAN: I don't know, my mouth? Where does anything come from? Where do crocodiles come from?

FREELANCER: Dinosaurs. But where do dinosaurs come from? And so on, down the ages. Until we're asking, "Where did nothing come from?" King Lear has an answer. King James has another.

MAN: I was just floating it out there. I don't know—somebody said "possibilities." *(Brief pause. Shaking his foot)* Man, my foot is totally asleep. It must be bored.

FREELANCER: This one culture whose name I forget thought the soul was in the feet. Other peoples have located it in the hands, or the eyes, the heart, all over the whole body.

SWEETHEART: "Peoples."

WOMAN: Yeah. *(Brief pause)* It's funny. The Soul. The Afterlife. We say words like that like we say words like Shoe and February. But, just honestly, just imagine, for one second.

MAN: It changes things. Life.

WOMAN: Mm-hmm. *(To Freelancer)* And it's like the thing you said. You don't know what the end is, so how can you know what you're in the middle of? They don't know what happens to you when you die, so how can they know, really, what happens to you when you're born?

FREELANCER: Or when you're in the middle. A serious mystery, then the middle part, then another mystery. Very good. *(He gestures that he'd like to write this down. To Woman)* May I?

WOMAN: Please. *(Freelancer writes)*

MAN: Hey, so, where's the husband, anyway? Is he supposed to represent something?

AUNT: Just a regular human being, I think. Maybe they have weekends together. People always figure something out. We're always scurrying around, looking over our shoulders, figuring something out. People. *(Brief pause)* We saw a play once that had an angel in it. A school production or some kind of community thing. Remember?

SWEETHEART: "Just a regular human being, I think."

WOMAN *(To Aunt)*: She is incredible. *(To Sweetheart)* You get everything word for word. It's a real gift. *(No response)*

FREELANCER: It's strange, though. It's like a museum exhibit about the last ten minutes. But it is—you're right, she's incredible. What a thing. Language, you know. Repeatability. Time, grammar, us. Weird.

WOMAN: Is, Was, Will be.

FREELANCER: That pretty much covers it. *(Brief pause)* I've been all over the world.

AUNT *(Musingly)*: "Is, Was, Will be."

WOMAN *(Nodding)*: Story of my life.

FREELANCER: I've seen so many things. Huh.

MAN *(Having noticed the armrest of his chair is loose)*: Look at this. *(He holds up the detached part)* This just comes completely off. *(He reattaches it)*

FREELANCER: All that travel, all the cathedrals and wonderful meals and evening light and people dying, and what are my findings? What's my conclusion? "Huh."

AUNT *(Looking in her purse)*: Usually I'll pack a little something to eat.

SWEETHEART: "Huh."

FREELANCER: Yeah. Exactly.

SWEETHEART: "People always look so worried."

FREELANCER: They do. Right. The cop said that.

SWEETHEART: People know what happens.

FREELANCER *(Wondering whom Sweetheart is quoting)*: Who said that?

AUNT *(Leafing through her program)*: People are born, people die. *(Patting Sweetheart on the knee)* We'll go to that nice place you like, after. We can do the treasure map on the placemat.

(The lights on the Intermission Audience dim three times, signaling the intermission has ended.)

And here we go. Exciting.

Lights down.

ACT TWO

———

Months later. Middletown.

Scene 1

Mechanic enters the dimly lit stage and comes to the window of John Dodge's house. John Dodge, illuminated, is staring out, intently. He cleans a piece of lint from the window, revealing that he was just staring at the pane of glass. Mechanic hides nearby, watching.

MECHANIC *(Imitating the sound of a crow)*: Ca-caa. Ca-caa.

> *(John Dodge barely reacts, except to shake his head in a very small way, as if quietly but deeply pained by the sound, and then moves from the window. Mechanic moves across stage, to where Mrs. Swanson, visible in her window, is looking at herself in a mirror. She is very pregnant. Mechanic makes a heavy long breathing sound:)*

Hhhhaaahh. Hhhhaaahh. *(Crow sound, again)* Ca-caa.

(Mrs. Swanson moves toward the window, looking frightened. Mechanic hides.)

MRS. SWANSON *(Muffled)*: Is someone there? *(She moves from the window)*

MECHANIC *(Steps out of his hiding place. To audience)*: Just some regular sounds from nature. Probably nothing to be too afraid of. *(Makes a few long whooshing sounds like the ocean or the wind in the trees)* Whhhshhhhhhh. Whhhshhhhhhh. That's my impression of a cell dividing—or, I don't know, metastasizing. Same thing, probably, for a while—until it isn't. I learned that word through relatives. *(Brief pause)* By the way, I started drinking, again. I don't know if people know that I'd stopped for a while? I did. Everything was better. But I decided to start up again. You might be asking yourselves, "Why?" *(Pause. He stays still and looks through the audience, suspiciously, but also with a kind of open curiosity)* That was a little chance to let your minds wander, to let you come up with some reasons for me. *(Another pause, same as above)* That was some time just for you. *(Takes a sip from a bottle)* Away! *(Pause. He slowly exits)*

Scene 2

Entrance and lawn of Middletown Hospital. Bright day. A sign that says EMERGENCY *is staked into the grass. Landscaper is on his knees on the grass, preparing to plant a tree, a young sapling. Cop enters and quietly approaches Landscaper from behind. Cop holds his hand out in the shape of gun, aimed at the back of Landscaper's head.*

COP: Bang!

LANDSCAPER *(Startled. Recovers)*: Jesus. Hey.

COP: I could have killed you, just then.

LANDSCAPER: And that's somehow my fault?

COP: Planting a tree?

LANDSCAPER: Great work—you solved the case of what I'm doing.

COP: Don't be smart.

LANDSCAPER: Done.

COP: How's my sister?

LANDSCAPER: She's good. She wants you to come over for dinner, next week. We finished the new patio and we're having a cookout. *(Some business with the tree)*

COP: Sounds good. *(Very brief pause)* What type is it? Elm?

LANDSCAPER: White Ash, I think. Although it could be a Green Ash. They're surprisingly hard to tell apart.

COP: Fair enough. *(Brief pause)* Pretty day.

LANDSCAPER *(Looking for a place to plant the tree)*: Where do you think this should go?

COP: A lot of possibilities. *(Brief pause. Shaking his head, contemplatively, somewhat disdainfully)* People.

LANDSCAPER: I know. *(Brief pause)* You know what, I don't know—what, specifically, about people?

COP: Just: people. The things they do. You think you know people. You don't. You think you caught some nonsuicidal gleam in their eye. You didn't. You never know what people are going to do.

(On Cop's lines above, Landscaper picks a spot on the grass, stands straight and still. Immediately after Cop has finished speaking, Landscaper gently sways for a few moments, his eyes closed, pretending he's a tree, making the sound of wind in the leaves.)

LANDSCAPER: Whhhshhhhhhh. Whhhshhhhhhh. This feels good, right here. What do you think about here?

COP: It's got potential.

LANDSCAPER *(Digging, preparing)*: So they just wheeled some guy past here. He lifted his head up, you know, "Wait, wait, one more look." That was a sight. Then a pregnant lady went in, crying, trying to carry all her stuff. She looked so lonely, which, you know, when you think about it, she totally isn't. It made me wish the thing was already done. I think it'll be soothing, you know, this tree, just nice for people. Bald kids going in on sunny school days. Shattered families leaving in the rain. Just a good old sturdy old tree. Year in, year out—a good tree.

COP: Sure.

LANDSCAPER: Maybe some day some young lovers'll carve their initials into it. *(He pinches the tree, not even an inch in diameter, with thumb and forefinger)* Into this. Pretty incomprehensible: the future.

COP: There are some guidelines, some givens.

LANDSCAPER: Yeah, maybe. *(He begins to dig)* I buried some sunglasses around back, this morning. Just to give somebody something to find, some day. *(He strikes something with the shovel)* Hey, what's that? *(Picks up the object, which is a rock)* I always think it's going to be gold or a skull or something. *(Brief pause. Holding up the rock)* Alas. That's got to be a really old word: "rock." *(He carefully sets the rock aside)*

COP: It fits pretty well, doesn't it.

LANDSCAPER: It sounds like a name the rocks would've picked out themselves. Same thing with "tree." *(He digs up another small rock and places it on top of the other and looks at the two rocks)* There. A monument to the moment of its own construction.

COP: A rock a person put on top of another rock.

LANDSCAPER: There's that word again. It's got a real honest ring to it: "rock." "Person," on the other hand, I'm not so sure. It feels sort of last-minute, doesn't it? Sort of fleeting? "Person."

COP: Sounds like an average-paying job.

LANDSCAPER: It does. "I'm a person. Been one for years, now. It's okay. The benefits, and so on. Of course, I'm not going to do it forever."

COP: This isn't really my kind of conversation.

LANDSCAPER: No?

COP: Yeah, not really. In fact, I've got to go in here. It's potentially a crime scene, if you can believe it. Tell my sister I said hi. I'll see you later. *(Exits, to enter the hospital)*

LANDSCAPER: See you later, person. I mean that in all the best ways. *(He digs up another rock, and places it on top of the others, making a tiny snowman or a semi-human statue)* Rock. Tree. *(He pokes in the dirt)* Worm. *(Stands up straight, leans on his shovel and sighs)*

Scene 3

Male Doctor's office. Mrs. Swanson and Male Doctor. Mrs. Swanson is very pregnant. Male Doctor, though entirely compassionate, is also very busy, and he speaks quickly. He is periodically writing, filling out forms, and referring to notes throughout this scene.

MALE DOCTOR: There's a problem—no, sorry, there's no problem. That's "Swenson." You're Swanson. Sorry. Now, we did some more tests on your little man. Everything looks very good. His Babinski reflex, for example.

MRS. SWANSON: Is that where you—

MALE DOCTOR *(Interrupting, nodding)*: Right—that's where we stroke the foot to see if the toes curl. We do this with sound and tiny beams of light. We can do almost all these tests prior to the actual birth, now. It's incredible. In a few more years, people won't even have to be born. Anyway, he was magnificent. The first expressive gesture. From that little curl of the toes to all of the world's Bibles and languages, it's just a matter of time. Everybody watched on the monitor. You probably heard a cheer go up from the other room. It's like a space launch. Long way away, but, he could be a tiny little Beethoven, your boy. Get him a fun little drum or a bell. Now, will the father be in the room with you?

MRS. SWANSON: He said he would, yes.

MALE DOCTOR: Good. It's good to have someone. This is literally going to be the first day of the rest of your baby's life. Linguistically, you'll want to start him out small. Simple words like hi and juice and tree and bye-bye. Say whatever you feel. Most of it happens on a vibrational level, anyway.

(A brief staticky buzz. A voice comes over the office intercom.)

INTERCOM: I'm sorry, Doctor—I have Mrs. Swenson on the line.

MALE DOCTOR *(Brief pause. To Intercom)*: Tell her I'm very sorry. I'll have to call her right back. *(To Mrs. Swanson)* Excuse me. That's a sad story. But, back to you. We'll generate a birth certificate, of course. That'll start up the paper trail. Do you have a name?

MRS. SWANSON: We're thinking possibly "John."

MALE DOCTOR: "John" is perfect. Biblical, one syllable, no complicated back-story, just "John." "John Swanson." It's like a little poem. *(Very brief pause)* What else?

MRS. SWANSON: Can I ask you . . . sorry, this is so general, but . . .
I mean, what should I do? How should I be?

MALE DOCTOR: Those are great questions. And here's my answer.
Love is all. It sounds so simple, I know, but, give him love.
Without it, he'll just go around the world saying different
things and seeing this and that and none of it'll make any dif-
ference. You've seen the type. Out in the rain, just kind of rat-
tling around in their bodies. But, it's easy. This is the time for
smiles and simple rhymes. Let's see you smile. *(Mrs. Swanson smiles. He barely smiles)* Great. Wow. Did you see? You
made me smile, too. Let's be honest, part of the whole great
March of Humanity is just swinging your arms and walking,
just smiling and moving forward. One other thing is: you
never know. So be forgiving, of yourself, of him, of nature,
everything. Nature is so insane, it's so rough, and we're just
humans, just these chatty mammals with different names and
colorful clothing. So, forgiveness, forgiveness and love, and
you're all set. Now, I'm speaking quickly, and I'm sure there's
a lot of huge gaps in my thinking. Apologies, I'm sorry,
I make this speech a lot.

MRS. SWANSON: No, no, it's great, it sounds completely unre-
hearsed. Thank you. I'm grateful for anything. It's good to
hear these things. *(She rubs her eye)*

MALE DOCTOR: Does your eye itch?

MRS. SWANSON: A little. Is that a problem?

MALE DOCTOR: Just for you. Because it itches.

MRS. SWANSON: Oh, right. Is there anything else I should do? In
the first little while?

MALE DOCTOR: Just hold him tight, hold the little human tight.
Sing as much as you can. After the first few weeks, the amni-
otic fluid will drain from his ears. Before that, mercifully,
everything is just a muffled kind of music. Same as in the
womb. Right now, to him, most words probably sound a

lot like the word "mother." Or "hearth" or "Earth," something indistinct like that, sort of rounded off. Who knows what shamanistic sense he's making of it all, you know? *(He speaks into her belly)* "Mahherhm. Herhomm. Mome gavnerma thurn." As far as he knows, the whole world is a soft little murmur of gentle intent. His instinct is going to be to trust life. His actual animal instinct—I never get over this—is to hold your hand. He's in there, right now, listening, forming, waiting to hold your hand. Wow, huh? Neither science nor religion has yet undone the wonder of the crying baby in air and light, grasping onto a finger.

MRS. SWANSON: You make it all sound so noble. Which it is, which I'm sure it is. *(Brief pause)* I'm sort of alone, in this, at the moment. I'm sort of afraid, sometimes. It's hard to believe so many women have done this before.

MALE DOCTOR: Oh, but they did. And they were scared. And they did great. So be scared. Be yourself. You look great. You look like someone's mother. Don't forget—it's so easy to forget, but—everyone in the world was born. Try to name someone who wasn't? You can't. So just be a part of the whole crazy thing. The rest is details, little tests, taps of a tiny hammer. Oh, take one of these. *(He hands her a tiny white cotton hat)* I get these free. Isn't it great? Did you ever see a tinier hat? Anyway, don't worry, why worry, come on, it's life. It's just good old life, been going on for years. *(Brief pause)* It's a lot, all at once, isn't it.

MRS. SWANSON: Well, it's just all sort of surreal.

MALE DOCTOR: It is. But it's also sort of real. But, you're right, it's strange. A little person inside you is going to come out of you.

MRS. SWANSON: It's almost vaudevillian.

MALE DOCTOR: It is, yes. *(He doesn't laugh)* That's very funny. But let's not overthink it. This is one time it makes good sense to just sit back and breathe and try to believe in miracles.

MRS. SWANSON: All right, I will. *(Brief pause)* What happens to you when you're born? *(Very brief pause)* Does it hurt?

MALE DOCTOR: Okay. Distress is certainly the first event. I'm sure there's a lot of pain, maybe even infinite pain, seeing as all we've known before has been infinite warmth. Even the gentlest birth must feel like a car crash. We'll probably never know the full effect. It could be the full effect is our life, our personality. Then it's over. He'll fall asleep in your arms, on your chest. He'll grasp your finger, because that's what the deepest thing in him tells him to do. It's so beautiful, it's so mysterious. You won't believe it. We have three.

MRS. SWANSON: Congratulations. That must be great.

MALE DOCTOR: It is. They are. My wife—her name is Jen—she said she forgot the pain, the worry, everything, the second she saw our firstborn. And she suddenly understood this word she'd been hearing all her life—Love. I felt it, too. You can't really describe it. As for the actual birth, we were worried, too, but, no surprises.

MRS. SWANSON: I'm glad. *(Brief pause)* What about yours?

MALE DOCTOR: What, my own birth? Oh. I don't know. I'm sure it was fine.

MRS. SWANSON: Were you close to your mother?

MALE DOCTOR: I don't know, yeah, you know—just regular mother and son. She's still with us. Great lady. *(Very brief pause)* What else, anything else?

MRS. SWANSON: I'm sure, but nothing I can think of.

MALE DOCTOR: I see you brought some stay-over things. Good. You're going to be great. Now, I'm sorry, please, excuse me. I really have to return this phone call. Go take a stroll. Walking is good. It's what we do. We hold hands and we walk. Activity can help the labor along. All right?

MRS. SWANSON: Thank you. Yes. Thanks.

MALE DOCTOR: Good. Perfect. Sorry I have to rush.

MRS. SWANSON: No, I appreciate your time. If I think of anything or if I have any—you're busy, sorry, thanks. Bye.

MALE DOCTOR: Great. Sorry. See you soon. *(Mrs. Swanson exits. Male Doctor begins looking through some paperwork)* Now, Swenson, Swenson . . . Swenson or Swanson? *(Quickly checks some other paperwork)* Swenson. One vowel away. Ahhhh. Eeee. Owww.

Scene 4

Hospital room. John Dodge is in bed. Female Doctor enters. Checks chart at the foot of the bed, etc.

FEMALE DOCTOR: How are you feeling?

JOHN DODGE: Okay, I think.

FEMALE DOCTOR: Good. *(Pause)* Sorry. This is difficult.

JOHN DODGE: I know. *(Brief pause)* What is?

FEMALE DOCTOR: Well, we don't know each other. Of course. So it's hard to know how to begin.

JOHN DODGE *(Pause)*: Are you going to try? *(Brief pause)* I know what you're thinking. I'm not this kind of person.

FEMALE DOCTOR: What kind of person?

JOHN DODGE: I'm normally just a face in the crowd. In fact, I'm normally just home, by myself. Just a face in my house. Which is fine, normally. I don't think that—I don't know.

FEMALE DOCTOR: Go ahead, what were you going to say?

JOHN DODGE: Maybe I'm imbalanced. Or, I was. But I don't think I'm suicidal, deep down. Even though, I mean, here I am, yes. And I think I'm probably making you feel uncomfortable.

FEMALE DOCTOR: I'm sure that's a little true. Thank you for your consideration. It's complicated.

JOHN DODGE: It is. I didn't know what I was doing. It was like this cloud came over me, this big dark idea.

FEMALE DOCTOR: And that was what?

JOHN DODGE: That I wanted to be an emergency, somehow. I always felt like one, deep down. I've got all these weird problems. I get nervous in certain weather. Sunlight reminds me of this great woman I knew. My heart races, I get these twitches in my elbow, my mind races. *(Brief pause)* It always scared me there was even a word: Suicide. It scared me they even had a word for it. And then, suddenly, there I am, you know, on my kitchen floor, like a crazy person, right in the thick of that word.

FEMALE DOCTOR: Forgive me, but, you used some kind of a knife?

JOHN DODGE: A house-painting tool. Like, a scraper thing.

FEMALE DOCTOR: That sounds dirty.

JOHN DODGE: What do you mean?

FEMALE DOCTOR: That it might have had dirt on it. Germs.

JOHN DODGE: Maybe. Probably. *(Pause)* I pictured everybody with their eyes all red, saying funeral stuff like, "We hardly knew him." And, in reality, they kind of didn't. I never thought I'd have a lonely life. I do, it turns out. Like, medically lonely. Like I've got sad genes. Like, what's that word? *(Very brief pause)* I don't know. I'm sure there is one.

FEMALE DOCTOR: I'm sorry.

JOHN DODGE: Please don't worry. I know I'm not crazy. I'm just sad. And not even that much, right now. I even feel hungry. That must be a good sign. *(Pause)* I keep explaining, but—I wanted to see if I had a survival instinct. It was a stupid way to find out, but I did. And I'm glad. And I'm better, I think. Not fine, but, better.

FEMALE DOCTOR: That's the thing.

JOHN DODGE: It really is. *(Brief pause)* What do you mean?

FEMALE DOCTOR: Well, we're not sure. Now, I just want to take a look at this.

(She puts on rubber gloves. She gently opens the surgical gauze covering the wound on his wrist.)

JOHN DODGE: It smells really bad.

FEMALE DOCTOR: That's bacteria. It could just be topical. But we're concerned. We're worried you might have something serious.

JOHN DODGE: Me?

FEMALE DOCTOR: An infection. We want to be cautious.

JOHN DODGE: Okay. Is "we" you and me?

FEMALE DOCTOR: All of us here. We might need to do a biopsy. I'll have them dress this again. *(She gently replaces the bandage)*

JOHN DODGE: Isn't there something you can give me?

FEMALE DOCTOR: We have you on an antitoxin named Neovitamole. *(Brief pause)* This is just a precaution, but, is there anyone you want us to contact?

JOHN DODGE *(Pause)*: Can you give me more of that stuff, just to make sure?

FEMALE DOCTOR: You're at the maximum. It's doing what it's going to do.

JOHN DODGE: What's it doing? What do I have?

FEMALE DOCTOR: I don't want to overwhelm you with details. You're showing signs of an infection, which we're trying to identify, and then, when we do, we can treat it.

JOHN DODGE: I'm having some trouble with my legs. And, my stomach's been . . . I've had diarrhea.

FEMALE DOCTOR: They told me. It can also strain the breathing, which is the big danger, if it's what we're worried about.

JOHN DODGE: It's curable, though, right?

FEMALE DOCTOR: We have high hopes on the Neovitamole. We'll see, fairly soon. It works quickly when it works. If not, there are other treatments. Some are somewhat radical, but they've been effective.

JOHN DODGE: What are they? No, forget it. You'll tell me when you tell me. *(Brief pause)* What happens when you die?

FEMALE DOCTOR: You don't need to think about dying.

JOHN DODGE: But what happens? Do you think.

FEMALE DOCTOR: A few things. Dying, from the outside, from the bodily perspective, it's not very pretty. Nobody looks very peaceful, as far as I've seen. We have stories of people seeing white light and feeling an angelic serenity. But these are stories from the people who lived, so they might be just describing what it's like to almost die and then live. So we don't know. *(Brief pause)* I was just speaking with a patient who's about to give birth.

JOHN DODGE: I guess that about covers it.

FEMALE DOCTOR: Those are just two events. There's a lot in between.

JOHN DODGE: I've always been afraid that shame would be the last thing I felt on Earth. No angelic stuff, no light—just weird pain, and shame that I was sick. And that I'd feel alone, no matter who was there. I've always been afraid of that. And now I just don't want to die like some dirty animal, with my teeth showing and some crazy look in my eye. *(Brief pause)* I'm sorry to talk like this.

FEMALE DOCTOR: No, it's good. In fact, we have someone here who's wonderful. Once we clear up this other thing, I think it'd be good for you to meet with her. Just to talk.

JOHN DODGE: I'd like that. *(Brief pause)* I guess this is a real irony. Me being here. How I got here.

FEMALE DOCTOR: Irony is a people thing. Nature is very frank. You're here, and we're taking care of you, is the point. Just this morning, my son, Eric, he's seven, said, "The sun doesn't know it's hot, right? It just goes around being orange."

JOHN DODGE: I don't want to die. God. I don't want to be in a hospital.

FEMALE DOCTOR: It's going to be okay.

JOHN DODGE: Oh, it is? For who? *(He becomes nauseous)* I'm getting this wave. I feel sick. I'm sorry. I think I'm going to be sick.

FEMALE DOCTOR: I can walk you to the bathroom, but it's better to stay still. *(She gets him a plastic bag)* Use this, if you need it.

JOHN DODGE: Is this the medicine or the thing?

FEMALE DOCTOR: The nausea? It could be both.

JOHN DODGE: When is it supposed to . . . God . . .

FEMALE DOCTOR: Just try to relax. Try to breathe. We're doing everything we can do.

JOHN DODGE: I don't want to be here. I don't want to be sick. *(Brief pause. The nausea is passing)* Okay. All right. I think I'm all right. Sorry. I'm sorry.

FEMALE DOCTOR: I'm going to get you something for your stomach. *(Referring to the call button by the bed)* Ring if you need anything or if there's any change.

JOHN DODGE: I made a mistake.

FEMALE DOCTOR: Don't worry about that. Just think ahead. Think about simple true things.

JOHN DODGE: Okay. I'll try. The sun is orange.

FEMALE DOCTOR: That's the spirit. Think of good things. I'll come through again soon. *(Exits)*

JOHN DODGE *(Trying not to cry)*: I'm thinking of good things.

Scene 5

Loading dock behind hospital. There are cardboard boxes and bags of garbage lying around. Mechanic is looking through them, examining little bits of trash. Female Doctor enters and stands on the raised loading dock.

MECHANIC: Sorry. *(He begins to leave)*

FEMALE DOCTOR: No, help yourself. I doubt there's anything good.

MECHANIC: I'm just looking around.

FEMALE DOCTOR: I used to smoke. I still come out here and just stand around for five minutes, thinking about cigarettes. Don't you volunteer, here?

MECHANIC: Yeah. I'm also a . . . I collect stuff.

FEMALE DOCTOR: Oh?

MECHANIC: Yeah. Just any kind of, like . . . honestly, I'm basically looking for some pills or something. Do you think there's anything in here for a headache? A serious one?

FEMALE DOCTOR: I don't, no.

MECHANIC: Probably not. You look important, up there. Like a person who saves lives. Very, you know—

FEMALE DOCTOR *(Interrupting)*: I'm not going to give you any pills.

MECHANIC: Oh. You still look—you know—you look really—

FEMALE DOCTOR *(Interrupting)*: Thank you. Careful you don't cut yourself. You can get botulism.

MECHANIC: That's a good name for a disease.

FEMALE DOCTOR: Isn't it. I always thought it sounded like a philosophy of really bad choices. People think it's not around anymore, botulism, but it is, it's alive and well.

MECHANIC: I'll be careful. *(Brief pause)* Today's my birthday.

FEMALE DOCTOR: Happy birthday. *(Nodding back toward hospital)* Someone's about to have a birthday in here.

MECHANIC: I guess it's pretty common. *(Brief pause)* I was a perfect baby.

FEMALE DOCTOR: I don't think I've ever heard anyone say that.

MECHANIC: Yeah. I just . . . I was all ready. For the world.

FEMALE DOCTOR: Surprise.

MECHANIC: Yeah.

FEMALE DOCTOR: It's not rare, but, it's very lucky—to be a person, just a regular person. Did you know when you combine an egg cell and a sperm cell, there's more ways they can combine, more particular kinds of people that can result, than there are atoms in the Universe?

MECHANIC: I love facts like that. *(Very brief pause)* I used to be seven pounds, eight ounces. Now look at me. *(Brief pause)* I think I disappointed everybody when I was born. If they'd just been expecting a little animal that needed air and food, then I think I would've been pretty impressive. There was no way I could live up to all that want and need, me and my seven pounds, eight ounces. I think being born hurt my feelings. *(Still looking around)* My head is killing me.

FEMALE DOCTOR: I'm sorry. *(Brief pause)* Can I ask you, this'll sound silly, but, what do you want out of life?

MECHANIC: Are you kidding?

FEMALE DOCTOR: Just for fun.

MECHANIC: Okay. I want, out of life, for this headache to go away. And, then, just, I guess, to know something. At the risk of sounding like some fuck-up pawing through the garbage for drugs: I want to know Love. I want to calmly know love on Earth. And to feel beautiful. *(Pause. He starts looking around, again. No trace of amusement)* Thanks. That was a lot of fun.

FEMALE DOCTOR: Pretty good answer. *(Brief pause)* I ask people sometimes and they say they don't know. You'd think we'd take the time. We have answers for so many things. How many atoms in the Universe, how black holes are made. *(Pause)* I'm sorry, I don't mean this to be embarrassing. *(She takes a vial of pills out of her jacket pocket, double-checks the label, then pours some on the ground)* Sometimes people spill things, back here. You're not driving, are you? *(He shakes his head no)* Happy birthday.

MECHANIC *(Picking up the pills)*: Yeah, you, too. Thanks.

Scene 6

Hospital room. John Dodge in bed. Attendant 2 enters and performs some routine task. She smiles at John Dodge, who smiles back, as she exits. Mrs. Swanson, on a stroll down the hall, appears at the door.

MRS. SWANSON: John? I don't believe it.

JOHN DODGE: Mary. Hi. Wow. Let me sit up. *(He lifts himself up in bed)*

MRS. SWANSON *(Laughing sympathetically)*: Oh, no. Look at you. What happened? *(She enters his room)*

JOHN DODGE: A couple things. Look at you. I could ask you the same thing.

MRS. SWANSON: This is so funny. I kept thinking I'd see you.

JOHN DODGE: I know. Me, too. I was always looking. I thought I saw you a couple times.

MRS. SWANSON: I almost called when it was so rainy. Remember all that rain? Our basement flooded.

JOHN DODGE: I almost called you, a few times. I'd, I don't know, I had really thought we'd have more of a relationship.

MRS. SWANSON: Well, we did. We do.

JOHN DODGE: Not a relationship, but, I mean, just, I don't know, I thought I'd see you.

MRS. SWANSON: And, here I am. Ta-da!

JOHN DODGE: I mean before. *(Brief pause)* You're so big. You look really great.

MRS. SWANSON: Today's the day, I hope. What about you? Are you okay?

JOHN DODGE: Yeah, no, I'm fine, it's just something stupid. I cut myself.

MRS. SWANSON: Making a birdhouse or a canoe or something? One of your projects?

JOHN DODGE: No, just, I don't know, around the house.

MRS. SWANSON: Do you have a cold?

JOHN DODGE: Do I sound stuffed up? I think I'm just tired. Good place to get some quiet, anyway.

MRS. SWANSON: I don't know how quiet it'll be for me.

JOHN DODGE: Oh, you'll be great. It's really nice to see you. Wow. *(Pause)* This is going to be dumb. Don't make fun of me.

MRS. SWANSON: What?

JOHN DODGE: Mary, sorry, can you hold me? Just for a—can I hold you?

MRS. SWANSON: I'm not sure how holdable I am. *(She sits on the bed)* But I can give you a hug.

(They hug. It's comforting to him, nice but slightly uncomfortable for her.)

JOHN DODGE: Mary.

MRS. SWANSON *(Stands)*: It's good to see you.

JOHN DODGE: It feels really good to see you. The people are nice here, but I don't really know anyone. So is your husband here?

MRS. SWANSON: Can you believe it, he isn't. He's trying to get a flight, right now. *(She notices his bandaged wrist)* Oh, no— you cut your hand? What did you do?

JOHN DODGE: It was stupid.

MRS. SWANSON: Oh, John—did you do this?

JOHN DODGE: Partly, yeah—I don't know. Yes.

MRS. SWANSON: Why? That's a stupid question, I'm sorry. But, why?

JOHN DODGE: I don't know. Nothing. A lot of things. It was a mistake.

MRS. SWANSON: God. I wish I'd known. I don't know what I could have done, but . . . I just wish . . .

JOHN DODGE: Yeah. I wanted to call. I don't know what I would've said. But, I'm all right. *(Brief pause)* If Bob doesn't make it, I can try to be there, in the delivery room. If you need someone.

MRS. SWANSON: That's really sweet. Thanks, John. I don't want to be alone in there. You're really thoughtful. *(Brief pause)* It might not be good, though, because you're . . . if it turns out you do have a cold.

JOHN DODGE: Okay. But, I don't think I do.

MRS. SWANSON: It's really nice of you to offer. *(Pause)* I'm sorry, I've got a lot on my mind.

JOHN DODGE: Yeah.

MRS. SWANSON: It's so good seeing you. They said activity was good. I was walking up and down the halls.

JOHN DODGE: I know, I can't believe it. *(Brief pause)* All these time. I mean, all these months.

MRS. SWANSON: The sink still drains like a dream. *(Brief pause)* Remember you unclogged our sink?

JOHN DODGE *(Long pause. He's dozed off. He opens his eyes. Quietly)*: Hey, Mary.

MRS. SWANSON: Hey. You need some rest. And, John, I should keep walking. They say activity is good.

JOHN DODGE: Sorry. God, I'm really tired. They've got me on this really serious stuff—it makes me so sleepy. *(Very brief pause)* It's so great that . . . Good old Mary.

MRS. SWANSON: Rest up and I'll see you soon, all right? Oh, here's some news, wait until you hear, you'll love this: we think we're going to name him John.

JOHN DODGE *(He hasn't heard)*: All right, Mary. It's really good to—I keep saying that, sorry. See you later, Mary. *(He begins to doze off again. She leaves the room)*

MRS. SWANSON: Bye, John.

(In the doorway, only partially visible to the audience, Mrs. Swanson doubles over.)

(In pain) Oh. Sorry? I think this is . . . John, can you call someone? Can you ring your call thing? John? *(He's asleep)* Someone? Somebody? I'm sorry, hello!?

(Attendant arrives, mainly out of view and out of earshot, and helps Mrs. Swanson off.

Pause. John Dodge gets out of his bed. Stands, turns, and faces out. He reaches for the bed, and steadies himself with it.)

JOHN DODGE: Was someone . . . hello? *(Brief pause)* Hey, I'm standing.

(Lights down.)

Scene 7

Entrance and lawn of Middletown Hospital.

The tree is planted. Mechanic, looking haggard, is sitting on a bench, staring at the pile of three rocks. He sips from a bottle in a paper bag. Librarian comes out of the hospital entrance.

LIBRARIAN: You've found a nice spot.

MECHANIC *(Referring to the rocks)*: I'm just looking at this.

LIBRARIAN: Maybe it's a sign.

MECHANIC: Maybe it isn't a sign. *(Pointing to sign that says EMERGENCY)* Maybe *this* is a sign.

LIBRARIAN: Maybe they're both signs. I'm here visiting a friend.

MECHANIC: I'm here, being difficult.

LIBRARIAN: You were always kind of a suspicious package. *(Brief pause)* I remember when you were little. Remember that? You wrote an essay for Middletown Day called "This Whole Hamlet Is Shaking." I had it hanging up at the library for years. I still remember the first sentence: "If this were . . ." No: "If Middletown was a horse instead of a town, it would be better for everyone and I would ride it off into the sun." Was that it?

MECHANIC: Wow. Yeah, that sounds right. It's always surprising when people remember something. I had to read it in front of everybody. I was shaking myself. It gave the thing an air of, like, I don't know—it made it more believable.

LIBRARIAN: I remember. They put your picture in the paper.

MECHANIC: Yeah. The color came out funny. All I was was the shape of a kid, with blurry teeth and hair.

LIBRARIAN: You could still tell you were happy. You looked very proud.

MECHANIC: I probably was. *(Brief pause)* I think someone scared my mother, before I was born, a lot. So all the blood I got was shaky blood. Jumpy blood from my jumpy mother. And so all I see is stupid shaky sad stuff and dark skies and sharp corners. And I want other people to enjoy the same experience. That's probably why I wrote that thing.

LIBRARIAN: I thought it was big of you. To stand up there and shake and say what you think and feel. We all have our ideas. Some people say the secret to life is being able to live in the middle of all our different ideas about life.

MECHANIC: Some people don't say anything.

LIBRARIAN: True.

MECHANIC: I didn't mean anything. Forget I said that.

LIBRARIAN: Okay. *(Brief pause)* My mother used to sing "You Are My Sunshine" to me, at night. And then she'd sing "Kentucky Moon" in the morning.

MECHANIC: That's nice. Mine was on her own. She tried and tried, I think. Just bad luck, I guess. A world full of fathers out there, but try to find one when you need one. I don't know. They do all their magic in the negative, anyway. My father was a speech impediment, is how I usually think of him. He came by once with a doll and some wrong-sized clothes.

LIBRARIAN: My father was very tall. He felt that posture was very important.

MECHANIC: Oh, yeah? *(Nodding toward hospital)* I forget, do they have food in there?

LIBRARIAN: There's a little snack bar. I had a good soup, the other day.

MECHANIC: It's weird. *(He takes a couple pills)* I've taken a lot of these. It's weird to be alive. I know it's supposed to be really important and great. But, here's my philosophy. I'm sitting on a bench. I'm wearing this shirt and these shoes. It's this certain weather. This is my body, end of story.

LIBRARIAN: I can't argue with that.

MECHANIC: Thank you. *(Pause)* Is this all right?

LIBRARIAN: Of course. I'm just here, waiting.

MECHANIC: Can I ask, did anyone ever explain things to you? Other than stuff about posture? Like, like, really sit down and just say, "Okay, You: here's how this whole thing works"?

LIBRARIAN *(Brief pause)*: There's an Indian prayer I always liked. I had it up on the wall, too: "If it's raining, it's not snowing. If it's snowing, the deer are thin. If the thin deer are sleeping, it is sunny. Hold the hand of your love and wait for the moon.

Some things we are never to know. Listen to the brook." It's sort of woodsy, but, I always liked it. I don't know if I have it word for word.

MECHANIC: It's nice. "Listen to the river." That's good. We did Indians in school. I did a reenactment. People clapped and my mom cried. That felt good. *(Brief pause)* There're people like me in the world, I think. You don't hear much from us because we usually don't say anything. But we're out here, trying to get a hold on the whole thing. It's like, I don't know, it's like trying to fix a moving car.

LIBRARIAN: I think we're born with questions and the world is the answer.

MECHANIC: Yeah? I guess there're a lot of different ways to go. Some people love God. I have a neighbor who kayaks every weekend. *(Pause)* You're not going to ask me what I want out of life, are you?

LIBRARIAN *(Shrugs and smiles, and shakes her head, as if to say: "I don't know, should I?")*

MECHANIC *(Pause. Close to crying)*: I just wish I got somewhere, you know? That I was born, and then I grew, somehow. I'd like people to look at me and feel wonder. I'd like people to look at me and say, "Wow. Look at that guy." I'd like to look at the sky and just think, "Hey, look at the sky." *(Pause)* What kind of soup was it?

LIBRARIAN: Tomato. Did you ever think you might be a normal person?

MECHANIC: Maybe. I don't know. Bad news for normal people. *(Brief pause)* I took a ton of those pills.

LIBRARIAN: Are you all right?

MECHANIC: Yeah.

(Cop enters from hospital entrance.)

COP: Hi, afternoon. *(To Mechanic)* You again, on a bench, again, with your pupils all constricted. You're Craig, right?

MECHANIC: Did you get a call to come down here and strangle me?

COP: Why would—no. They want you in there.

MECHANIC: Why don't you like me?

COP *(To Librarian)*: What's this?

LIBRARIAN: He's not feeling well. Be gentle.

COP *(Brief pause)*: Okay. Craig, I'm sure you'll be fine. You've been really good about showing up for these. They want you in there, okay?

MECHANIC: Okay. *(He slowly gets up, begins to enter hospital. To Librarian)* Good luck with your friend. *(Exits)*

LIBRARIAN: Bye, Craig. Thank you.

COP: I think he wrote the dirty word on the sign coming into town. I'm sorry, I never liked his attitude. Like he's too good to do the stuff everyone has to do. Like he's always thinking there's somewhere better to be than here.

LIBRARIAN: Maybe there is. A lot of people probably feel that, sometimes.

COP: Maybe. Probably. Ah, God, I don't know—I'm sorry. I don't even know the guy. I guess I'm not feeling very patient.

LIBRARIAN: I'm sorry about your mother, Robert.

COP: Thanks, Judith. Thanks for coming.

LIBRARIAN: You made a beautiful speech.

COP: I didn't prepare anything. I thought I'd just go up there and talk.

LIBRARIAN: Well, it was lovely. Everyone cried and felt so close to her.

COP: I almost cried. I had a hard time not crying.

LIBRARIAN: You were a good son.

COP *(Brief pause)*: It was hard. They had her on everything, at the end, so she wasn't very clear. She did these things with her hands. My sister thinks she was playing piano in her mind. Remember she used to teach music? It made us happy to think that's what was happening, that she was playing some song in her head. We were happy she had things to do, even though there was nothing to do in there.

LIBRARIAN: It was good you could be with her. She was a wonderful woman.

COP: She was almost our oldest resident. *(Brief pause)* A few days before, I was here visiting, and she asked me, "What does this actually mean?" and she held up her middle finger. It was so funny. I said, "Mom, where'd you see that?" It was on some show that had couples working out their problems. She couldn't work the remote to turn it off. But, so, I told her it means, "I don't like you." Then I felt so terrible, almost sick, for even saying those words to my mom, even though I was just explaining. I just wanted to get her flowers and make her laugh and help her get back home and feel peaceful.

LIBRARIAN: I'm sure she knew how you felt. That's a sweet story. *(Pause)* People know what happens.

COP: Yes, they do.

LIBRARIAN: It seems so original, when it happens to us.

COP: I like the natural order of things, but, yeah, it's hard. When we were leaving, after, her doctor said, "See you later." My sister and I had a laugh about that, over breakfast. Yes, we shall. Sorry—how are you?

LIBRARIAN: I'm fine, thank you. *(Brief pause)* Mary Swanson is supposed to be having her baby, today.

COP: From over on Oak Street, right? Number 31?

LIBRARIAN: Yes. Mary. That's funny—is that how you remember people?

COP: What? The address? Yeah, I guess. Just a habit. If I know the address, the general layout, then I can sympathize. *(Brief pause)* Toward the end, I sat with my mom and we listed stores we'd been to. Isn't that sad, that one day, there's going to be a last store you ever went into?

LIBRARIAN: It is. But isn't it great to think there was a first? *(She thinks for a moment)* Frank's Superette.

COP: Frank's Superette.

LIBRARIAN *(Brief pause)*: Look at this pretty tree.

COP: Yeah. It's nice. I like trees. Everybody does, I'm sure, but, yeah, me, too. *(Brief pause)* I should get back in here. Will you be at the library tomorrow?

LIBRARIAN: I will.

COP: I'll come in and say hi.

LIBRARIAN: I'll say hi back.

COP: Thanks, Judith. Thanks. *(Enters the hospital)*

Scene 8

Mrs. Swanson's hospital room. Mrs. Swanson is in bed. Attendant enters with a pitcher of water.

ATTENDANT: Make sure you drink some water. Even if you're not thirsty. *(Does some quick business, chart-checking, etc.)*

MRS. SWANSON: Okay.

ATTENDANT: How are you? *(Pause)* Can I get you anything?

MRS. SWANSON: Oh, sorry. No. Thank you. I was just thinking about everything.

ATTENDANT: That's good to do, sometimes. And sometimes it's good to just look out a window. Everything's going to be fine. I'll be up again with some food in just a bit.

MRS. SWANSON: Food.

ATTENDANT: Not hungry?

MRS. SWANSON: I don't know. I'm just kind of . . . God.

ATTENDANT: You're kind of God? Very nice to meet you—love your work. It'll all come back, your appetite and everything. *(Checking her forehead for fever)* Do you feel all right, otherwise?

MRS. SWANSON: I just thought everything would be different.

ATTENDANT: And it isn't?

MRS. SWANSON: People had trouble with travel arrangements. My husband and one of my brothers. Whatever was going to happen, I just didn't think I'd be alone.

ATTENDANT: They'll get here. Don't feel alone. You're not alone. Just rest. *(Motioning toward a call button)* Ring, okay. If you need anything.

MRS. SWANSON: I will, thanks. *(Attendant exits)* I'm not alone.

Scene 9

John Dodge's hospital room. John Dodge is lying in bed. Cop enters, respectfully.

JOHN DODGE *(Somewhat scared and confused. His voice is slightly hoarse)*: I'm sorry. Am I not supposed to be—

COP *(Interrupting)*: It's okay. Hi. I'm Sergeant Hollingsworth. I don't know if you remember, I came to your house when the ambulance was there.

JOHN DODGE: Sorry, I thought I was in the wrong room. *(Brief pause)* I remember. It was busy, but I remember you.

COP: I wanted to let you know there won't be any charges filed here. The arrangement is you'll do some community service when you get better and that you'll agree to get some help, some counseling.

JOHN DODGE: Thank you.

COP: Does that sound all right?

JOHN DODGE: Have you talked to them, here?

COP: No. Why?

JOHN DODGE: I don't know.

COP: Does it sound all right?

JOHN DODGE: Okay.

COP *(Puts some papers by the bed)*: Look at these. They need to be signed. The address to send them to is up at the top. Are you feeling better?

JOHN DODGE: I think I'm losing my voice.

COP: Well, you were a real mess. *(Brief pause)* You look better.

JOHN DODGE: Did you tell Stephanie?

COP: Who's Stephanie?

JOHN DODGE: I don't know. I'm sorry. She's from when I was little. *(Brief pause)* I don't hear any voices in my head. Should I be hearing any voices?

COP: Are you all right?

JOHN DODGE: I think so.

COP: Just rest up and listen to your doctors.

JOHN DODGE: I will.

COP: Life can get tough. It's tough for everyone. You know that, right?

JOHN DODGE: Yeah.

COP: I get moody. I get sad. People don't think of cops as moody. *(Gesturing toward his gun, notebook, flashlight, etc.)* Look at all this stuff I have to walk around with.

JOHN DODGE: It's a lot of stuff. *(Brief pause)* I just want to be a regular living person.

COP: You will. I have to be back for something else, tomorrow. I'll stop in.

JOHN DODGE: Stephanie is from when I was little. I was little.

COP: Stephanie. Okay. *(Brief pause)* I'll have them stop in and check on you, okay? Have a look at those papers and send them back.

JOHN DODGE: Are you leaving?

COP: Yeah, I've got to go. See you later.

JOHN DODGE: Okay.

COP: So, one part of the community service thing is managing the community garden on West Street. Building little stuff and just making sure everything's all taken care of. They said you're good with stuff like that.

JOHN DODGE: Yeah, I like stuff like that.

COP: Well, then, get better. I think they give you a uniform or something.

JOHN DODGE: That'd be good. I like working outside.

COP: All right, then. I'll see you later. *(Exits)*

JOHN DODGE: Bye.

Scene 10

Mrs. Swanson's room. Mrs. Swanson sitting up in bed. Warm light. Female Doctor enters with the tiny baby, swaddled in a blanket.

MRS. SWANSON *(With nothing but love)*: Ohhh.

FEMALE DOCTOR *(Gently hands the baby to Mrs. Swanson)*: Somebody needs you.

MRS. SWANSON: I missed him so much. Was he fussing?

FEMALE DOCTOR: He just wants his mommy. *(She pulls up the blanket, to cover the baby, who makes a small sound)* Take the cloth off him. There you go. As much skin-to-skin contact as possible. Just let him feel you holding him. Look at you both. You're like a Renaissance painting.

MRS. SWANSON: He feels so nice.

FEMALE DOCTOR: Everything's fine. He's a very healthy baby.

MRS. SWANSON: Oh, good. Lucky boy. My lucky healthy boy.

FEMALE DOCTOR: I'll leave you two.

MRS. SWANSON: Thanks, Julie. Thank you. *(Female Doctor exits. Softly)* Johnnie. There you go. That's nice. Hello, John. Easy. Hello. Welcome to the world, little boy. How does it feel? I wonder what you're feeling. There you go. Ssshhh. What are you feeling on Earth?

Scene 11

Follows quickly on Scene 10. John Dodge's hospital room. John Dodge is lying in bed. Occasional sounds of labored breathing. Suddenly, he goes into small convulsions. A muffled and very congested scream. His movements are small, but grotesque. It is protracted, irregular, difficult to watch. He's dying like an animal. A desperate look toward the audience and then he is still. Lights down.

Scene 12

Follows fairly quickly on Scene 11. Mrs. Swanson and the body of John Dodge are visible, though in darkness, on the stage. The playing area should be unspecific, empty. Mechanic enters, partly dressed as a Chakmawg Indian, with headdress, war paint, bells attached to his boots. His movements are somewhat slow but precise. He begins a ceremonial American Indian chant, in the tradition of the Apache or Sioux. It's haunting and beautiful and strange in melody. It slowly builds in intensity, as he becomes more possessed and more convinced of his expressiveness. He continues, to his physical and emotional limit. Pause.

ATTENDANT *(Enters)*: Craig?

MECHANIC *(This line is spoken indistinctly)*: I was beautiful.

ATTENDANT: Did you just say you were beautiful? *(Mechanic nods)* Well, then, I'm sure you were. Everything fits okay? *(Pause. He nods)* You're going to be in pediatric, today. The kids love to see the Rain Dance. Just move around, ring the bells. I don't know if you did any of the reading I gave you? Just be spiritual. Don't use "to be" verbs. No is, was, or, will be. Too many tenses gets confusing. They're just kids. Keep it simple. You know? "It rain and children grow strong, like tree. Sun cross sky many time. Brave and squaw laugh, touch noses. Life never die. This land never die." Something like that. Sound good? They'll love it. Okay? *(Brief pause)* Did you just wake up? Are you okay?

MECHANIC: Yeah.

ATTENDANT: Are you going to be all right? *(He nods)* All right. You'll be great. They're just kids. Smile and walk in circles and they see the history of the world. They're just like us, except smaller. Okay?

MECHANIC: Yeah.

ATTENDANT: Okay. Me go do some filing. Me want leave early, play tennis, before sun go away. Thanks, Craig. *(She exits)*

MECHANIC *(Looks into the audience. Pause)*: Me.

Scene 13

John Dodge's hospital room. Lights up on the body of John Dodge, on the bed, under a sheet. Attendant and Attendant 2 are taking care of the room, unplugging equipment, etc. Lights will remain up on the body, throughout the rest of the play.

ATTENDANT: The coroner is on his way.

ATTENDANT 2: Dr. Elliman? He's nice.

ATTENDANT: His son goes to school with my daughter.

ATTENDANT 2 *(Referring to a file that's hanging at the foot of the bed)*: Does this stay with the patient?

ATTENDANT: Yeah.

ATTENDANT 2: It's so quiet.

ATTENDANT: I think bodies soak up sound. Listen. *(To John Dodge's body)* We are in a room. You are a body. I am wearing these clothes. *(To Attendant 2)* Do you notice that? *(Again, to John Dodge's body)* This is the sound of my voice. This is the language I use. You are far away. Where are you? What are you feeling? Test—one, two. *(Brief pause. To Attendant 2)* It sounds funny, doesn't it.

ATTENDANT 2: I guess. It's weird. Did you talk to him, before?

ATTENDANT: A little. He was worried about a library book. He was sad but he tried to be good-natured.

ATTENDANT 2: I came in once to change something and he said, "If I had flowers, I'd give them to you."

ATTENDANT: That's sweet. *(One last bit of business)* I think that does it. *(She checks a schedule)* Now I think we have to go up to five. *(They exit. Attendant 2 lingers by the door)*

ATTENDANT 2 *(To John Dodge's body)*: Good-bye, person. That was nice about the flowers. I hope you're not sad.

Scene 14

Mrs. Swanson's hospital room. She is lying in bed with the baby on her chest, under the covers. Librarian is sitting by the bedside. There is a radio in the room.

COP *(Enters. Quietly)*: Hello. Are you . . . is everyone dressed? Hi. Congratulations. I'm Robert Hollingsworth. Judith was telling me. I'm really happy for you. I'm over on Pine Street, near the river.

MRS. SWANSON: Thank you, Robert. I'm Mary Swanson.

LIBRARIAN: He's a beautiful boy. Just perfect. He's sleeping.

COP: That's the life.

MRS. SWANSON: Thank you for visiting. It's nice to have people.
(Small sound from the baby as she readjusts him on her chest)

COP: Yeah, no, of course. I had to be down here, anyway.

(Sweetheart, from Intermission Audience, enters.)

Hello, Sweetheart. How did you get up here? Are you lost?

SWEETHEART: No.

MRS. SWANSON: Do you want to look? *(She folds back the blanket a little)*

SWEETHEART *(Comes closer and leans in to look at the baby)*: Hi.

MRS. SWANSON: He says, Hello. He says, How are you?

SWEETHEART: Fine.

LIBRARIAN: Well. This has been quite a day. *(Brief pause. Looking at the baby)* He looks so peaceful. *(Sweetheart takes a glance across the stage to the body of John Dodge)*

COP: Yeah. *(To Mrs. Swanson)* Why don't we . . . we should let you be.

LIBRARIAN: Yes, you should rest up.

COP *(Exiting with Sweetheart)*: Congratulations, again.

LIBRARIAN: There's a radio. Would you like some music?

MRS. SWANSON: That might be nice.

LIBRARIAN: I'll leave you this and you can find something. *(She gives Mrs. Swanson a remote control)* Okay, darling. I'll see you tomorrow. *(Exits)*

MRS. SWANSON *(To the baby)*: Those were our neighbors. *(She turns on the radio. It's a program about science)*

RADIO: "... with a mass more than three times the weight of the sun, of such gravity that it collapses into a black hole. The structure of a black hole is very simple. There is the surface, and the center, or singularity, from which no light can escape. If my friend Sally could watch from a safe distance beyond the event horizon and see me fall into a black hole, what would she see? Sally would see me falling, slower and slower. It would appear that I'll never quite reach the center. If I were waving, she would see me wave, slower and slower. 'Bye, Sally.' *(Janitor enters John Dodge's room, rolling a large trash can on wheels. He empties the trash can at the foot of John Dodge's bed)* For me, the fall would only take a short time. Years would pass, where she was. Eventually, it would look to her as if I had stopped, mid-fall. She would see my hand in the air, my flailing legs, my smile, all frozen—all motion would stop for her. This is because the light from me takes so long to escape. Finally, it will cease altogether. By then, Sally's great-great-grandchildren will be very old people. And I will still be falling, will still be waving good-bye. Next week, we'll visit with a giant tortoise who has an interesting story to tell, if he could speak. He's over a hundred years old! We'll also talk with a man and woman who doubt almost everything they've ever"—

(Mrs. Swanson changes radio stations with the remote control. On the new station the last minute or so of the choral part of Beethoven's Ninth Symphony is playing. After about fifteen or twenty seconds, Attendant 2 enters to refill a water pitcher. Attendant 2 gives a little wave to the baby, and then exits. Mrs. Swanson listens to the end. A sedate female voice comes on:)

"That was the Symphony Number Nine, in a recording from 1981 of the Philharmoniker"—

(Mrs. Swanson turns radio off. Janitor enters.)

JANITOR: Evening.

MRS. SWANSON: Hello.

JANITOR: Don't mind me. *(He empties the trash)* Wow, is that a baby?

MRS. SWANSON: This is John.

JANITOR: Excellent. Congratulations.

MRS. SWANSON: Thank you.

JANITOR: John's a good name.

MRS. SWANSON: Thank you.

JANITOR: I guess they all are, when you think about it. *(A small sound from the baby)* Hey, he's trying to talk. *(Last bit of janitorial work)* Is the temperature all right in here?

MRS. SWANSON: Yes, thank you, it's fine.

JANITOR: Good. Okay, see you later. *(Exits)*

MRS. SWANSON: Bye. *(To baby)* Say bye. Say bye-bye.

(A pause. Lights fade.)

END

CHARACTERS

(in order of appearance)

PUBLIC SPEAKER	male, 40s–60s
COP	male, 30s–50s
MRS. SWANSON	female, late 30s
JOHN DODGE	male, late 30s–40s
MECHANIC	male, late 20s–30s
LIBRARIAN	female, 50s–60s
TOUR GUIDE	female, 20s–30s
MALE TOURIST	30–40s
FEMALE TOURIST	30–40s
GREG	male, 40s–60s

Intermission Audience:

AUNT	female, 40s–50s
SWEETHEART	female, 12–16
FREELANCER	male, 30s–40s
MAN	20s–30s
WOMAN	20s–30s

LANDSCAPER	male, 20s–30s
MALE DOCTOR	40s–50s
FEMALE DOCTOR	40s–50s
ATTENDANT #2	female, 20s–30s

| ATTENDANT | female, 20s–30s |
| JANITOR | male, 30s–50s |

Also, offstage voices of:

COP'S RADIO	female
GROUND CONTROL	
(possibly seen onstage)	male
INTERCOM	female
RADIO HOST (science show)	male
RADIO HOST	
(classical music show)	female

There is much opportunity for double-casting of roles, but this should be done as unobtrusively as possible, and not for the purpose of commenting on the nature of any of the characters.

Stage Sets

Act One

Window of the Swanson house and window of John Dodge's
   house
Town square
Library
Space
The Swanson kitchen
Seating for Intermission Audience

Act Two

Window of the Swanson house and window of John Dodge's
   house

Entrance and lawn of Middletown Hospital

Doctor's office

John Dodge's hospital room

Loading dock behind hospital

Mrs. Swanson's hospital room

A natural and unforced symmetry might exist between aspects of the sets in the first act and second act. Specifically, between the Swanson and Dodge houses, in the first, and the Swanson and Dodge hospital rooms, in the second; and between the town square and the hospital lawn and entrance.

Production History

On November 3, 2010, *Middletown* received its world premiere production at the Vineyard Theatre (Douglas Aibel, Artistic Director; Jennifer Garvey-Blackwell, Executive Director) in New York City. It was directed by Ken Rus Schmoll; the set design and costume design were by David Zinn, the lighting design was by Tyler Micoleau, the sound design was by Jill BC DuBoff; the properties master was Lily Fairbanks, the production stage manager was Charles M. Turner III. The cast was:

PUBLIC SPEAKER	David Garrison
COP	Michael Park
MRS. SWANSON	Heather Burns
JOHN DODGE	Linus Roache
MECHANIC	James McMenamin
LIBRARIAN	Georgia Engel
TOUR GUIDE	McKenna Kerrigan
MALE TOURIST	Ed Jewett
FEMALE TOURIST	Cindy Cheung
GREG	David Garrison

Intermission Audience:

AUNT	Johanna Day
SWEETHEART	Olivia Scott

FREELANCER	Ed Jewett
MAN	Pete Simpson
WOMAN	Cindy Cheung
LANDSCAPER	Pete Simpson
MALE DOCTOR	David Garrison
FEMALE DOCTOR	Johanna Day
ATTENDANT #2	Cindy Cheung
ATTENDANT	McKenna Kerrigan
JANITOR	Pete Simpson

Offstage voices of:

COP'S RADIO	Johanna Day
GROUND CONTROL (possibly seen onstage)	Pete Simpson
INTERCOM	Johanna Day
RADIO HOST (science show)	Ed Jewett
RADIO HOST (classical music show)	McKenna Kerrigan

In June 2011, *Middletown* will receive a production at Steppenwolf Theatre Company (Martha Lavey, Artistic Director; David Hawkanson, Executive Director) in Chicago. At the time this book went to print, the cast and artistic team were to be as follows: direction, Les Waters; set design, Antje Ellerman; costume design, Janice Pytel; lighting design, Matt Frey; sound design and music composition, Richard Woodbury; dramaturg, Rebecca Rugg; stage manager, Laura D. Glenn. The roles of Mrs. Swanson, Female Tourist, Man, Woman, Landscaper, Attendant, Janitor, Cop's Radio and Ground Control were not yet assigned. The cast:

PUBLIC SPEAKER	Tim Hopper
COP	Francis Guinan
JOHN DODGE	Tracy Letts

MECHANIC	Michael Patrick Thornton
LIBRARIAN	Martha Lavey
TOUR GUIDE	Alana Arenas
MALE TOURIST	Tim Hopper
GREG	Tim Hopper

Intermission Audience:

AUNT	Ora Jones
SWEETHEART	Alana Arenas
FREELANCER	Tim Hopper

MALE DOCTOR	Tim Hopper
FEMALE DOCTOR	Ora Jones
ATTENDANT #2	Alana Arenas

Offstage voices of:

INTERCOM	Alana Arenas
RADIO HOST (science show)	Tim Hopper
RADIO HOST (classical music show)	Ora Jones

Acknowledgments

Thank you to the Vineyard Theatre, Steppenwolf Theatre, and Portland Center Stage. And to Mark Subias, great friend and agent. And to Gordon Lish, great friend and teacher. And to Don DeLillo, Noy Holland, and Edward Albee. And Kathy Sova. And James Hogan and Oberon Books. My high opinion of human beings is without doubt due to the existence and example of the great friends, above and below. Thank you to Ty Burrell, Joe Sola, Danny Wolohan, Rainn Wilson, Alex Kitnick, and other members of the Department of Sanitation Tennis Club. Jeff Greene, Shevaun Mizrahi, Jean Strouse, Bret Gladstone, Sam Lipsyte, Sam Michel, Michael Kimball, Constance Wu, James Urbaniak, and Les Waters. What great names. And such great people. Doris Kim, Lauren Hutton, Hal Brooks, Rachel Hicks, Saxon Palmer, Christopher Grallert, Mark Rossier, and my sister Madeleine. Thank you for helping me and it to be all right.

—W.E.